Homestyle Cas

Ground Beef, Chicken, Vegetables & More!

S. L. Watson

DEDICATION

To my mother who could make a casserole out of anything!

CONTENTS

Introduction

Casseroles are a weeknight staple in my house. Most recipes are easy and quick to prepare. Included are a wide variety of recipes so most any taste will be satisfied. I can easily fix a casserole and put dinner in the oven while I prepare the rest of the meal. Included are recipes for ground beef, ham, sausage, Italian sausage, chicken, turkey, meatless meals and vegetables. Homestyle casseroles are hearty, filling and are great for lunch the next day. Casseroles are a budget friendly and tasty way to use up leftovers.

Homestyle vegetable casseroles are a delicious way to use fresh, frozen or canned vegetables. We all need to add vegetables to our diet but they just taste so much better in a hot and hearty casserole.

Hiding vegetables in casseroles is a great way to introduce them to picky eaters.
It is not always easy to fix dinner with a busy life and trying to feed the family what they will eat. This cookbook is full of family style recipes for cauliflower, spinach, broccoli, green beans, asparagus, eggplant, corn, squash and more. The recipes use everyday ingredients for easy vegetable meals and side dishes for your family.

On meatless nights, I fix two vegetable casseroles and serve them with fresh fruit. The casseroles are hearty and you will not miss the meat.

1 GROUND BEEF

Ground beef is the most common meat used in casseroles. I love creamy casseroles, Mexican and Italian casseroles using ground beef. Homestyle casseroles are hearty and filling. Add a few frozen or fresh ingredients and you can have a casserole ready in no time.

Potato Taco Casserole

Makes 4 servings

1 1/2 cups dry mashed potato flakes
1 1/4 cups water
1 cup sour cream
1 lb. ground beef
1 envelope taco seasoning mix
1 cup shredded cheddar cheese
1 cup shredded lettuce
1 cup chopped tomatoes
2 cups corn chips

Preheat the oven to 350°. In a mixing bowl, add the potato flakes, 1/2 cup water and sour cream. Stir until combined. Press the potatoes in the bottom of a 9 x 13 casserole dish. Bake for 20 minutes or until the potatoes are lightly browned around the edges. Remove the dish from the oven but leave the oven on.

In a skillet over medium heat, add the ground beef. Stir frequently to break the ground beef into crumbles as it cooks. Cook for 8 minutes or until the ground beef is well browned and no longer pink. Drain off any excess grease. Add the taco seasoning mix and 3/4 cup water to the skillet. Stir constantly and bring the water to a boil. Reduce the heat to low and simmer the ground beef for 10 minutes. Remove the skillet from the heat.

Spoon the ground beef over the potatoes. Sprinkle the cheddar cheese over the ground beef. Bake for 5 minutes or until the cheese melts. Remove the dish from the oven. Sprinkle the lettuce, tomatoes and corn chips over the top before serving.

Beefy Taco Bake with Cheddar Biscuits

Makes 4 servings

1 lb. lean ground beef
1 envelope taco seasoning mix
1 cup chunky salsa
2 cups frozen whole kernel corn
2 cups Bisquick
1 cup shredded cheddar cheese
2/3 cup whole milk

In a skillet over medium heat, add the ground beef. Stir frequently to break the ground beef into crumbles as it cooks. Cook for 8 minutes or until the ground beef is well browned. Drain all the excess grease from the skillet.

Add the taco seasoning mix, salsa and corn to the skillet. Stir constantly and cook until the ground beef is boiling. Remove the skillet from the heat and spoon the ground beef into an 8" square baking pan.

Preheat the oven to 425°. In a mixing bowl, add the Bisquick, cheddar cheese and milk. Stir until a soft dough forms. Drop the dough, by tablespoonfuls, onto the ground beef. Bake for 20 minutes or until the biscuits are tender and golden brown. Remove the dish from the oven and serve.

Southwest Beef and Tater Tot Casserole

Makes 6 servings

1 lb. ground beef
2 tsp. chili powder
1 tsp. ground cumin
2 cups frozen green beans, thawed
10.75 oz. can cream of mushroom soup
3/4 cup whole milk
14 oz. can diced tomatoes, drained
1 1/2 cups cooked whole kernel corn
1/4 cup chopped green bell pepper
3 cups frozen tater tots

In a large skillet over medium heat, add the ground beef. Stir frequently to break the ground beef into crumbles as it cooks. Cook for 8 minutes or until the ground beef is well browned and no longer pink. Drain any excess grease from the ground beef.

Add the chili powder and cumin to the skillet. Stir constantly and cook for 2 minutes. Add the green beans, cream of mushroom soup, milk, tomatoes, corn and green bell pepper. Stir constantly and cook until the soup comes to a boil. Remove the skillet from the heat.

Spoon the casserole into a 9 x 13 casserole dish. Place the tater tots over the top of the casserole. Preheat the oven to 350°. Bake for 50 minutes or until the tater tots are crispy and the casserole bubbly. Remove the casserole from the oven and serve.

Cheesesteak Casserole

Makes 6 servings

1 1/2 tsp. dried minced onion
1 lb. lean ground beef
3/4 cup jarred cheese dip
2 cups Bisquick
1 cup whole milk
1 egg
1 cup chopped onion
1 cup chopped green bell pepper
1/2 cup shredded cheddar cheese

In a large skillet over medium heat, add the minced onion and ground beef. Stir frequently to break the ground beef into crumbles as it cooks. Cook for 8 minutes or until the ground beef is well browned and no longer pink. Drain off the excess grease. Add the cheese dip to the skillet. Stir constantly and cook for 5 minutes.

In a mixing bowl, add the Bisquick, milk and egg. Stir until well blended. Spray an 8" square baking pan with non stick cooking spray. Pour half the batter into the pan. Spoon the ground beef filling over the batter. Sprinkle the onion and green bell pepper over the ground beef. Pour the remaining batter over the ground beef.

Preheat the oven to 375°. Bake for 40 minutes or until the batter is done and golden brown. Sprinkle the cheddar cheese over the top of the dish. Bake for 5 minutes. Remove the dish from the oven and serve.

Italian Meat and Potatoes Casserole

Makes 8 servings

1 lb. lean ground beef
1 cup chopped onion
1/4 tsp. salt
24 oz. jar tomato and basil pasta sauce
4 cups prepared mashed potatoes
16 oz. jar Parmesan & mozzarella cheese sauce
1 cup shredded mozzarella cheese

In a skillet over medium heat, add the ground beef and onion. Stir frequently to break the ground beef into crumbles as it cooks. Cook for 8 minutes or until the ground beef is well browned and no longer pink. Remove the skillet from the heat and drain off any excess grease. Stir the pasta sauce into the ground beef.

Preheat the oven to 350°. Spray a 9 x 13 casserole dish with non stick cooking spray. Spoon the ground beef into the casserole dish. In a mixing bowl, add the mashed potatoes and cheese sauce. Stir until combined and spread over the top of the ground beef. Bake for 30 minutes. Sprinkle the mozzarella cheese over the top of the casserole. Bake for 5 minutes or until the cheese melts and the casserole is hot and bubbly. Remove the casserole from the oven and serve.

Baked Bean Casserole

Makes 8 servings

1/2 lb. ground beef
8 slices bacon, cooked and crumbled
1 cup chopped onion
1/2 cup light brown sugar
1/4 cup ketchup
1/4 cup barbecue sauce
2 tbs. yellow prepared mustard
2 tbs. molasses
1/2 tsp. chili powder
1 tsp. salt
1/2 tsp. black pepper
15 oz. can kidney beans, rinsed and drained
15 oz. can pinto beans, rinsed and drained
2 cans pork and beans, 15 oz. size

In a skillet over medium heat, add the ground beef. Stir frequently to break the meat into crumbles as it cooks. Cook for 6 minutes or until the ground beef is well browned and no longer pink. Remove the skillet from the heat and drain all the excess grease from the ground beef.

Preheat the oven to 350°. Spray a 9 x 13 casserole dish with non stick cooking spray. Add the ground beef, bacon, onion, brown sugar, ketchup, barbecue sauce, mustard, molasses, chili powder, salt, black pepper, kidney beans, pinto beans and pork and beans with liquid to the dish. Stir until combined.

Bake for 1 hour or until the dish is bubbly and most of the liquid absorbed. Remove the dish from the oven and serve.

Taco Cornbread Bake

Makes 6 servings

1 lb. ground beef
1 envelope taco seasoning mix
1/2 cup water
15 oz. can whole kernel corn, drained
1/2 cup chopped green bell pepper
1 cup tomato sauce
8 oz. pkg. cornbread muffin mix
3 oz. can french fried onions
1/3 cup shredded cheddar cheese

In a skillet over medium heat, add the ground beef. Stir frequently to break the meat into crumbles as it cooks. Cook for 7 minutes or until the ground beef is well browned and no longer pink. Drain off any excess grease.

Add the taco seasoning mix, water, corn, green bell pepper and tomato sauce to the skillet. Stir until well combined and the filling is thoroughly heated. Remove the skillet from the heat.

Spray a 2 quart casserole dish with non stick cooking spray. Spoon the ground beef filling into the dish. Prepare the cornbread muffin mix batter according to package directions. Stir half the french fried onions into the cornbread batter. Spoon the batter, by tablespoonfuls, over the top of the casserole.

Preheat the oven to 400°. Bake for 20 minutes or until the cornbread is done and the casserole bubbly. Sprinkle the remaining french fried onions over the casserole. Sprinkle the cheddar cheese over the casserole. Bake for 3 minutes. Remove the dish from the oven and serve.

Tortilla Chip Beef Casserole

Makes 6 servings

1 1/2 lbs. ground beef
10.75 oz. can cream of chicken soup
2 1/2 cups crushed tortilla chips
2 cups salsa
1 1/2 cups shredded cheddar cheese

In a skillet over medium heat, add the ground beef. Stir frequently to break the ground beef into crumbles as it cooks. Cook for 10 minutes or until the ground beef is well browned and no longer pink. Remove the skillet from the heat and drain off the excess grease. Add the cream of chicken soup to the skillet. Stir until combined.

Preheat the oven to 350°. Spray a shallow 2 1/2 quart casserole dish with non stick cooking spray. Spread 1 1/2 cups tortilla chips in the bottom of the casserole dish. Spread the ground beef over the chips. Spread the salsa over the ground beef. Sprinkle the cheddar cheese over the top.

Bake for 30 minutes or until the casserole is hot and bubbly. Sprinkle 1 cup tortilla chips over the top of the casserole. Bake for 3 minutes. Remove the dish from the oven and serve.

Chili Cheese Potato Tots Casserole

Makes 8 servings

2 lbs. ground beef
1 cup chopped onion
2 cans chili without beans, 15 oz. size
14 oz. can petite diced tomatoes
15 oz. can Mexicorn, drained
2 cups shredded Colby Jack cheese
32 oz. pkg. frozen tater tots

In a large skillet over medium heat, add the ground beef and onion. Stir frequently to break the ground beef into crumbles as it cooks. Cook for 10 minutes or until the ground beef is well browned and no longer pink. Remove the skillet from the heat and drain all the grease from the ground beef.

Stir in the chili, tomatoes with juice and Mexicorn. Preheat the oven to 350°. Spray a 9 x 13 casserole dish with non stick cooking spray. Spoon the ground beef filling into the dish. Sprinkle the Colby Jack cheese over the top. Spread the tater tots over the top.

Bake for 1 hour or until the tater tots are golden brown and the casserole bubbly. Remove the dish from the oven and serve.

Potato Beef Casserole

Makes 4 servings

1 lb. ground beef
1 cup chopped onion
1 cup chopped green bell pepper
4 potatoes, peeled and sliced
10.75 oz. can cream of chicken soup
10.50 oz. can condensed vegetable beef soup
1/2 tsp. salt

In a skillet over medium heat, add the ground beef, onion and green bell pepper. Stir frequently to break the ground beef into crumbles as it cooks. Cook for 8 minutes or until the ground beef is well browned. Remove the skillet from the heat and drain all the grease from the skillet.

Spray a 3 quart casserole dish with non stick cooking spray. Preheat the oven to 350°. Add the ground beef, potatoes, cream of chicken soup, vegetable soup and salt to the dish. Stir until combined. Cover the dish with a lid or aluminum foil. Bake for 1 hour or until the potatoes are tender. Remove the dish from the oven and serve.

Hearty Potato Beef Casserole

Makes 4 servings

1 lb. ground beef
1 onion, thinly sliced
1 diced green bell pepper
1 tbs. unsalted butter
4 peeled potatoes, cut into 1/2" cubes
2 tomatoes, seeded and chopped
10.75 oz. can cream of chicken soup
1/4 cup chili sauce
3/4 tsp. salt
1/4 tsp. black pepper
1/4 cup grated Parmesan cheese

In a skillet over medium heat, add the ground beef, onion, green bell pepper, butter and potatoes. Stir frequently to break the ground beef into crumbles as it cooks. Cook for 10 minutes or until the ground beef is well browned and the potatoes tender. Remove the skillet from the heat. Drain off the excess grease.

Add the tomatoes, cream of chicken soup, chili sauce, salt and black pepper to the skillet. Stir until combined. Spray a 9 x 13 casserole dish with non stick cooking spray. Preheat the oven to 350°. Spoon the ground beef filling into the dish. Bake for 15 minutes. Sprinkle the Parmesan cheese over the top of the casserole. Bake for 10 minutes or until the casserole is hot and bubbly. Remove the dish from the oven and serve.

Cheesy Beef Casserole

Makes 6 servings

1 lb. ground beef
3/4 cup chopped onion
2 cups tomato sauce
1/2 tsp. garlic powder
1/2 tsp. salt
1/4 tsp. black pepper
8 oz. cream cheese, softened
1 cup cottage cheese
3/4 cup grated Parmesan cheese
8 cups cooked egg noodles
1/3 cup sliced green onion
1/4 cup chopped green bell pepper

In a large skillet over medium heat, add the ground beef and onion. Stir frequently to break the ground beef into crumbles as it cooks. Cook for 8 minutes or until the ground beef is well browned. Drain off any excess grease.

Add the tomato sauce, garlic powder, salt and black pepper to the skillet. Stir until combined and remove the skillet from the heat. In a mixing bowl, add the cream cheese, cottage cheese and 1/2 cup Parmesan cheese. Stir until combined.

Preheat the oven to 350°. Spray a 9 x 13 casserole dish with non stick cooking spray. Place half the noodles in the casserole dish. Spoon half the ground beef over the noodles. Spread half the cream cheese mixture over the ground beef. Repeat the layering process one more time using the remaining noodles, ground beef and cream cheese mixture.

Cover the dish with a lid or aluminum foil. Bake for 40 minutes or until the casserole is hot and bubbly. Remove the lid or aluminum foil. Sprinkle 1/4 cup Parmesan cheese, green onion and green bell pepper over the top of the casserole. Bake for 5 minutes. Remove the dish from the oven and serve.

Cheesy Beef and Rice Casserole

Makes 6 servings

1 lb. ground beef
1 cup dry long grain rice
1 garlic clove, minced
2 tbs. unsalted butter
3 cups water
2 carrots, shredded
2 tsp. instant beef bouillon granules
1 tsp. dried parsley flakes
1/2 tsp. salt
1/2 tsp. dried basil
1/2 tsp. dried minced onion
1 cup shredded cheddar cheese

In a large skillet over medium heat, add the ground beef. Stir frequently to break the ground beef into crumbles as it cooks. Cook for 8 minutes or until the ground beef is well browned and no longer pink. Remove the skillet from the heat and drain all the excess grease from the skillet. Remove the ground beef from the skillet and set aside.

Place the skillet back on the heat. Add the rice, garlic and butter. Stir constantly and cook the rice for 5 minutes. Add the water, carrots, beef bouillon, parsley, salt, basil and onion. Stir until combined and bring the rice to a boil. Place a lid on the skillet and simmer the rice for 5 minutes. Remove the skillet from the heat and stir in the ground beef.

Preheat the oven to 325°. Spray a 9" square baking dish with non stick cooking spray. Spoon the casserole into the dish. Cover the dish with a lid or aluminum foil. Bake for 45 minutes or until the rice is tender. Remove the lid or aluminum foil. Sprinkle the cheddar cheese over the top of the casserole. Bake for 5 minutes. Remove the dish from the oven and serve.

Sloppy Joe Hashbrown Bake

Makes 8 servings

1 1/2 lbs. lean ground beef
15 oz. can sloppy joe sauce
15 oz. can chili with beans
4 cups frozen shredded hashbrowns
2 cups shredded cheddar cheese

In a large skillet over medium heat, add the ground beef. Stir frequently to break the meat into crumbles as it cooks. Cook for 8 minutes or until the ground beef is well browned and no longer pink. Drain any excess grease from the ground beef.

Add the sloppy joe sauce and chili to the skillet. Stir until combined and remove the skillet from the heat. Preheat the oven to 425°. Spray a 9 x 13 casserole dish with non stick cooking spray. Spread the ground beef filling over the bottom of the casserole dish. Spread the hashbrowns over the top. Place a lid or aluminum foil on the casserole dish. Bake for 30 minutes.

Remove the lid or aluminum foil and bake for 10 minutes. Sprinkle the cheddar cheese over the top. Bake for 10 minutes. Remove the dish from the oven and serve.

Polenta Casserole

Makes 6 servings

1 cup plain yellow cornmeal
1 tsp. salt
4 cups water
1 lb. ground beef
1 cup chopped onion
1/2 cup chopped green bell pepper
2 garlic cloves, minced
14 oz. can diced tomatoes
1 cup tomato sauce
4 cups sliced fresh mushrooms
1 tsp. dried basil
1 tsp. dried oregano
1 tsp. dried dill
1/8 tsp. Tabasco sauce
1 1/2 cups shredded mozzarella cheese
1/4 cup grated Parmesan cheese

In a mixing bowl, add the cornmeal, salt and 1 cup water. Stir until combined. In a sauce pan over medium heat, add 3 cups water. When the water is boiling, add the cornmeal. Stir constantly and cook for 4 minutes or until the cornmeal thickens. Reduce the heat to low. Place a lid on the pan and simmer the cornmeal for 15 minutes. Remove the pan from the heat.

Spray two 8" square baking pans with non stick cooking spray. Spread the polenta into the pans. Refrigerate the polenta for 1 1/2 hours or until the polenta is cold and firm.

In a large skillet over medium heat, add the ground beef, onion, green bell pepper and garlic. Stir frequently to break the ground beef into crumbles as it cooks. Cook for 8 minutes or until the meat is well browned and no longer pink. Drain off any excess grease.

Add the tomatoes, tomato sauce, mushrooms, basil, oregano, dill and Tabasco sauce to the skillet. Stir until combined and bring the sauce to a boil. When the sauce is boiling, reduce the heat to low. Simmer the meat sauce for 20 minutes. Remove the skillet from the heat.

Spread half the meat sauce over the polenta in each pan. Sprinkle 3/4 cup mozzarella cheese over the meat sauce. Sprinkle 1/8 cup Parmesan cheese over the top of each casserole.

Cover the pans with a lid or aluminum foil. Preheat the oven to 350°. Bake for 40 minutes. Remove the lid or aluminum foil from the pans. Bake for 15 minutes or until the casserole is hot and bubbly. Remove the casserole from the oven and serve.

Spicy Nacho Casserole

Makes a 9 x 13 casserole dish

1 lb. ground beef
1 1/2 cups chopped onion
1 1/4 cups chopped green bell pepper
28 oz. can diced tomatoes
15 oz. can hot chili beans
15 oz. can black beans, rinsed and drained
11 oz. can whole kernel corn, drained
1 cup tomato sauce
1 envelope taco seasoning mix
1/8 tsp. cayenne pepper
13 oz. bag spicy nacho tortilla chips
2 cups shredded cheddar cheese

In a dutch oven over medium heat, add the ground beef, onion and green bell pepper. Stir frequently to break the ground beef into crumbles as it cooks. Cook for 10 minutes or until the ground beef is no longer pink and well browned. Drain all the grease from the skillet.

Add the tomatoes with juice, chili beans with liquid, black beans, corn, tomato sauce, taco seasoning mix and cayenne pepper to the pan. Stir constantly and bring the mixture to a boil. Reduce the heat to low and cook for 30 minutes. Remove the pan from the heat.

Preheat the oven to 350°. Spray a 9 x 13 casserole dish with non stick cooking spray. Place half the tortilla chips in the bottom of the casserole dish. Spoon half the ground beef mixture over the chips. Place the remaining chips over the ground beef. Spoon the remaining ground beef over the chips. Sprinkle the cheddar cheese over the top of the casserole. Bake for 30 minutes. Remove the dish from the oven and serve.

Beef and Bean Nacho Casserole

Makes 6 servings

1 lb. lean ground beef
1 tbs. taco seasoning mix
1/2 cup spicy French dressing
10.75 oz. can condensed fiesta nacho soup
14 oz. can Mexican style diced tomatoes
15 oz. can pinto beans, drained and rinsed
1 1/2 cups shredded cheddar cheese
2 cups crushed Doritos chips
1 cup shredded lettuce
1/4 cup sliced black olives

In a skillet over medium heat, add the ground beef. Stir frequently to break the ground beef into crumbles as it cooks. Cook for 8 minutes or until the ground beef is well browned and no longer pink. Drain any excess grease from the ground beef.

Add the taco seasoning mix, French dressing and fiesta nacho soup to the skillet. Stir until combined and cook until the soup is bubbly. Remove the skillet from the heat.

Preheat the oven to 375°. Spoon the ground beef into an 8" square baking pan. Drain the tomatoes and spread over the ground beef. Spoon the pinto beans over the tomatoes. Sprinkle the cheddar cheese over the top of the dish. Cover the dish with a lid or aluminum foil. Bake for 30 minutes.

Remove the lid or aluminum foil from the dish. Bake for 10 minutes. Remove the dish from the oven. Sprinkle the Doritos, lettuce and black olives over the top of the casserole before serving.

Enchilada Bake

Makes 6 servings

1 cup chopped tomatoes
1 1/2 cups cooked whole kernel corn
1/4 cup red bell pepper, chopped
10 oz. can enchilada sauce
1 lb. ground beef
1 envelope taco seasoning mix
1/4 cup water
4 cups tortilla chips
2 cups shredded cheddar cheese
1/4 cup sliced green onion

Spray a 2 quart casserole dish with non stick cooking spray. In a mixing bowl, add the tomatoes, corn, red bell pepper and enchilada sauce. Stir until well combined.

In a skillet over medium heat, add the ground beef. Stir frequently to break the ground beef into crumbles as it cooks. Cook for 8 minutes or until the ground beef is well browned and no longer pink. Drain any excess grease from the ground beef. Add the taco seasoning mix and water to the ground beef. Stir constantly and cook for 4 minutes. Remove the skillet from the heat.

Spread half the ground beef in the casserole dish. Place 1 1/2 cups tortilla chips over the ground beef. Sprinkle 1/2 cup cheddar cheese over the chips. Spread half the tomato mixture over the chips. Repeat the layering process one more time.

Sprinkle the remaining cup cheddar cheese over the top of the casserole. Sprinkle the green onion over the top. Place the remaining tortilla chips around the edges of the casserole. Preheat the oven to 375°. Bake for 30 minutes or until the dish is hot and bubbly. Remove the casserole from the oven and serve.

Mexican Beef, Bean and Rice Casserole

Makes a 9 x 13 casserole dish

1/2 lb. ground beef
1 tsp. ground cumin
1/2 cup chopped green bell pepper
1/2 cup chopped red bell pepper
1/2 cup chopped onion
1/2 cup cooked brown rice
15 oz. can whole kernel corn, drained
14 oz. can diced tomatoes
4 oz. can diced green chiles, drained
15 oz. can pinto beans, rinsed and drained
2 tbs. chili powder
Tabasco sauce to taste
1 cup shredded cheddar cheese
1 cup sour cream

In a large skillet over medium heat, add the ground beef, cumin, green bell pepper, red bell pepper and onion. Stir frequently to break the meat into crumbles as it cooks. Cook for 8 minutes or until the ground beef is well browned and no longer pink. Remove the skillet from the heat and drain off the excess grease.

Preheat the oven to 350°. Spray a 9 x 13 casserole dish with non stick cooking spray. Add the ground beef mixture, brown rice, corn, tomatoes with juice, green chiles, pinto beans and chili powder to the casserole dish. Stir until combined. Season to taste with Tabasco sauce. Sprinkle the cheddar cheese over the top of the dish.

Bake for 20 minutes or until the casserole is hot and bubbly. Remove the dish from the oven and spoon dollops of sour cream over the top.

Beefy Rice Casserole

Makes 4 servings

1 lb. ground beef
1/2 cup chopped onion
1/4 cup chopped celery
1/4 cup chopped green bell pepper
2 cups cooked rice
1 cup sliced fresh mushrooms, cooked
8 oz. can tomato sauce
1/2 cup ketchup
5 bacon slices, cooked and crumbled
1 tsp. salt
1/8 tsp. black pepper

In a large skillet over medium heat, add the ground beef, onion, celery and green bell pepper. Stir frequently to break the ground beef into crumbles as it cooks. Cook for 10 minutes or until the ground beef is well browned and no longer pink. Drain any excess grease from the ground beef.

Add the rice, mushrooms, tomato sauce, ketchup, bacon, salt and black pepper to the skillet. Stir until combined and bring the casserole to a boil. Remove the skillet from the heat.

Preheat the oven to 350°. Spoon the casserole into a 2 quart casserole dish. Bake for 40 minutes. Remove the casserole from the oven and serve.

Beefy Eggplant & Feta Ziti

Makes 8 servings

1 lb. ground beef
6 cups eggplant, peeled and cubed
1/2 cup chopped onion
1 garlic clove, minced
4 cups spaghetti sauce
1/4 tsp. ground cinnamon
4 cups cooked ziti pasta
8 oz. feta cheese with garlic & herbs, crumbled
2 cups shredded mozzarella cheese

In a large skillet over medium heat, add the ground beef, eggplant, onion and garlic. Stir frequently to break the ground beef into crumbles as it cooks. Cook for 10 minutes or until the ground beef is well browned and the eggplant tender. Drain all the excess grease from the skillet. Stir in the spaghetti sauce and cinnamon. Stir frequently and cook for 5 minutes. Remove the skillet from the heat.

Preheat the oven to 375°. Spray a 9 x 13 casserole dish with non stick cooking spray. Place half the ziti noodles in the bottom of the casserole dish. Spoon half the ground beef and eggplant over the noodles. Sprinkle half the feta and mozzarella cheese over the ground beef. Repeat the layering process one more time using the remaining ziti, ground beef and eggplant and cheeses.

Bake for 30 minutes or until the casserole is hot and bubbly. Remove the dish from the oven and cool for 10 minutes before serving.

Chinese Burger Casserole

Makes 6 servings

1 lb. ground beef
2 cups diced onion
1 cup diced celery
1 cup dry long grain rice
1 cup sliced cooked mushrooms
28 oz. can Chinese vegetables, drained
1/4 cup soy sauce
1 1/2 cups water
10.75 oz. can cream of mushroom soup
10.75 oz. can cream of chicken soup
1 cup chow mein noodles

In a large skillet over medium heat, add the ground beef, onion and celery. Stir frequently to break the ground beef into crumbles as it cooks. Cook for 8 minutes or until the ground beef is well browned and no longer pink. Remove the skillet from the heat and drain all the excess grease from the skillet.

Add the rice, mushrooms, Chinese vegetables, soy sauce, water, cream of mushroom soup and cream of chicken soup to the skillet. Stir until combined. Spray a 9 x 13 casserole dish with non stick cooking spray. Preheat the oven to 350°. Spoon the casserole into the dish. Cover the dish with a lid or aluminum foil. Bake for 30 minutes.

Remove the lid or aluminum foil from the dish. Sprinkle the chow mein noodles over the top. Bake for 30 minutes or until the casserole is bubbly and the rice tender. Remove the dish from the oven and serve.

Cabbage Roll Casserole

Makes 12 servings

2 lbs. ground beef
1 1/4 cups chopped onion
3 garlic cloves, minced
2 cans tomato sauce, 15 oz. size
1 tsp. dried thyme
1/2 tsp. dried dill
1/2 tsp. rubbed sage
1/4 tsp. salt
1/4 tsp. black pepper
1/4 tsp. cayenne pepper
2 cups cooked rice
4 bacon slices, cooked and crumbled
9 cups shredded cabbage
1 cup shredded mozzarella cheese

In a large skillet over medium heat, add the ground beef, onion and garlic. Stir frequently to break the ground beef into crumbles as it cooks. Cook for 10 minutes or until the ground beef is well browned and no longer pink. Drain off the excess grease.

Add 1 can tomato sauce, thyme, dill, sage, salt, black pepper and cayenne pepper to the skillet. Stir until combined and bring the sauce to a boil. When the sauce is boiling, reduce the heat to low. Simmer for 5 minutes. Stir in the rice and bacon. Remove the skillet from the heat.

Preheat the oven to 375°. Spray a 9 x 13 casserole dish with non stick cooking spray. Spread 3 cups cabbage in the bottom of the casserole dish. Spread 1/2 the ground beef sauce over the cabbage. Spread 3 cups cabbage over the ground beef. Spread the remaining ground beef sauce over the cabbage. Sprinkle 3 cups cabbage over the top of the beef. Spread the remaining can tomato sauce over the top of the casserole. Cover the dish with a lid or aluminum foil. Bake for 45 minutes.

Remove the lid or aluminum foil from the dish. Sprinkle the mozzarella cheese over the top and bake for 10 minutes. Remove the dish from the oven and serve.

Meatball Macaroni and Cheese Casserole

Makes 4 servings

12 cups water
3 cups dry rotini pasta
8 oz. pkg. frozen Italian style meatballs
2 1/4 cups whole milk
1 envelope dry white sauce mix
1 cup shredded cheddar cheese
1 cup shredded mozzarella cheese
1 tbs. melted unsalted butter
3 tbs. Italian seasoned breadcrumbs
2 chopped green onions

In a large sauce pan over medium heat, add the water. When the water is boiling, add the rotini pasta. Cook for 7 minutes or until the pasta is tender. Remove the pan from the heat and drain all the water from the pasta.

Preheat the oven to 350°. Spray a 2 quart casserole dish with non stick cooking spray. Add the meatballs and pasta to the dish. In a sauce pan over medium heat, add the milk and white sauce mix. Stir constantly and cook until the sauce thickens and bubbles. Add the cheddar cheese and mozzarella cheese to the pan. Stir until the cheese melts. Remove the pan from the heat and pour the sauce over the meatballs and noodles. Stir until all the ingredients are combined.

In a small bowl, stir together the butter, breadcrumbs and green onion. Sprinkle the breadcrumbs over the top of the dish. Bake for 30 minutes or until the casserole is bubbly and the breadcrumbs golden brown. Remove the dish from the oven and serve.

Chili Casserole

I keep the ingredients on hand for this easy casserole all the time. Teenagers love it and always want me to make it.

Makes 6 servings

3 cans Hormel beef chili with beans, 15 oz. size
4 oz. can diced green chiles, drained
1/2 cup sliced black olives
2 cups shredded cheddar cheese
4 cups Doritos, crushed

Spray a 2 1/2 quart casserole dish with non stick cooking spray. Preheat the oven to 350°. Add all the ingredients to the casserole dish. Stir until combined. Bake for 30 minutes or until the casserole is bubbly. Remove the dish from the oven and serve.

Salsa Chili Mac Casserole

Makes 6 servings

1 lb. pkg. dry elbow macaroni
1 lb. ground beef
2 cups salsa
10 oz. Velveeta cheese, cubed
15 oz. can chili style beans

In a dutch oven over medium heat, add the elbow macaroni. Cover the macaroni with water and bring the macaroni to a boil. Cook for 6 minutes or until the macaroni is tender. Remove the pan from the heat and drain all the water from the macaroni.

In a skillet over medium heat, add the ground beef. Stir frequently to break the ground beef into crumbles as it cooks. Cook for 6 minutes or until the ground beef is well browned. Drain off the excess grease. Add the salsa, Velveeta cheese and beans with liquid to the skillet. Stir constantly and cook until the cheese melts. Remove the skillet from the heat and add to the macaroni. Stir until combined.

Preheat the oven to 350°. Spray a 9 x 13 casserole dish with non stick cooking spray. Pour the macaroni into the baking dish. Bake for 30 minutes or until the casserole is hot and bubbly. Remove the dish from the oven and serve.

Cowboy Casserole

Makes 6 servings

1 lb. ground beef
16 oz. can baked beans, drained
1/2 cup barbecue sauce
2 cups Bisquick
2/3 cup whole milk
1 tbs. softened unsalted butter
1/2 cup shredded cheddar cheese

In a large skillet over medium heat, add the ground beef. Stir frequently to break the ground beef into crumbles as it cooks. Cook for 8 minutes or until the ground beef is well browned. Drain any excess grease from the ground beef.

Add the baked beans and barbecue sauce to the skillet. Stir constantly and cook until the ground beef is bubbly. Remove the pan from the heat and spoon the ground beef into a 2 quart casserole dish.

Preheat the oven to 425°. In a mixing bowl, add the Bisquick, milk and butter. Stir until a soft dough forms. Drop the dough, by tablespoonfuls, onto the hot filling. Bake for 20 minutes or until the biscuits are golden brown and the casserole bubbly. Sprinkle the cheddar cheese over the biscuits. Bake for 3 minutes. Remove the dish from the oven and serve.

Spaghetti Casserole

Makes a 9 x 13 casserole dish

1 1/2 lbs. ground beef
1 green bell pepper, chopped
1 onion, chopped
14 oz. can diced tomatoes
1 cup tomato sauce
1 tbs. light brown sugar
1 tsp. salt
1 tsp. chili powder
1/2 tsp. black pepper
1/4 tsp garlic powder
1/8 tsp. cayenne pepper
6 cups cooked spaghetti noodles
3/4 cup shredded cheddar cheese

In a large skillet over medium heat, add the ground beef, green bell pepper and onion. Stir frequently to break the ground beef into crumbles as it cooks. Cook for 10 minutes or until the ground beef is well browned and no longer pink. Drain all the grease from the skillet.

Add the tomatoes with juice, tomato sauce, brown sugar, salt, chili powder, black pepper, garlic powder and cayenne pepper to the skillet. Stir until combined and cook for 1 minute. Remove the skillet from the heat.

Preheat the oven to 350°. Spray a 9 x 13 casserole dish with non stick cooking spray. Add the noodles and ground beef to the casserole dish. Stir until combined. Sprinkle the cheddar cheese over the top. Bake for 35 minutes. Remove the dish from the oven and serve.

Pizza Noodle Casserole

Makes a 9 x 13 casserole dish

2 lbs. ground beef
1/4 cup chopped onion
2 jars pizza sauce, 15 oz. size
10.75 oz. can condensed cheddar cheese soup
10 oz. pkg. egg noodles, hot and cooked
2 cups shredded mozzarella cheese

In a skillet over medium heat, add the ground beef and onion. Stir frequently to break the ground beef into crumbles as it cooks. Cook for 10 minutes or until the ground beef is well browned and no longer pink. Remove the skillet from the heat and drain the excess grease from the ground beef.

Add the ground beef, pizza sauce, cheddar cheese soup and egg noodles to a 9 x 13 casserole dish. Stir until well combined. Preheat the oven to 350°. Bake for 30 minutes. Sprinkle the mozzarella cheese over the top of the casserole. Bake for 15 minutes or until the casserole is hot, bubbly and the cheese melted. Remove the casserole from the oven and cool for 5 minutes before serving.

Zucchini Beef Casserole

Makes 6 servings

1 lb. ground beef
1/2 cup chopped onion
1/2 tsp. salt
1/8 tsp. black pepper
2 cups thinly sliced zucchini
1 cup chopped tomato
3/4 cup dry long grain rice
1 cup water
19 oz. can tomato basil vegetable soup
2 cups shredded mozzarella cheese

In a skillet over medium heat, add the ground beef and onion. Stir frequently to break the ground beef into crumbles as it cooks. Cook for 8 minutes or until the ground beef is well browned and no longer pink. Drain any excess grease from the ground beef. Sprinkle the salt and black pepper over the ground beef. Remove the skillet from the heat and stir in the zucchini and tomato.

Preheat the oven to 375°. Spray a 9 x 13 casserole dish with non stick cooking spray. Add the rice and water to the casserole dish. Spoon the ground beef and vegetables over the rice. Pour the tomato basil soup over the top of the dish. Do not stir. Cover the dish with a lid or aluminum foil. Bake for 40 minutes or until the rice is tender.

Remove the lid or aluminum foil. Sprinkle the mozzarella cheese over the top of the casserole. Bake for 15 minutes. The casserole should be hot and bubbly and the mozzarella cheese melted when ready. Remove the casserole from the oven and serve.

Ground Beef Spinach Casserole

Makes 8 servings

1 1/2 lbs. ground beef
2 garlic cloves, minced
1/2 tsp. salt
1/2 tsp. black pepper
26 oz. jar spaghetti sauce
1 tsp. dried Italian seasoning
10 oz. pkg. chopped frozen spinach, thawed and drained
2 cups shredded Monterey Jack cheese
1 1/2 cups sour cream
1 egg, beaten
1 tsp. garlic salt
4 cups wide egg noodles, hot and cooked
1 1/2 cups shredded Parmesan cheese

In a dutch oven over medium heat, add the ground beef, garlic, salt and black pepper. Stir frequently to break the ground beef into crumbles as it cooks. Cook for 8 minutes or until the ground beef is well browned and no longer pink. Drain off any excess grease. Stir in the spaghetti sauce and Italian seasoning. Remove the pan from the heat.

Stir in the spinach, Monterey Jack cheese, sour cream, egg and garlic salt. Stir until all the ingredients are combined. Gently fold in the egg noodles. Spray a 9 x 13 casserole dish with non stick cooking spray. Spoon the casserole into the casserole dish. Sprinkle the Parmesan cheese over the top.

Preheat the oven to 350°. Bake for 30 minutes or until the casserole is hot and bubbly. Remove the dish from the oven and serve.

Corned Beef Casserole

Serve this casserole with coleslaw and sliced tomatoes for a delicious and easy dinner.

Makes 6 servings

1/4 cup unsalted butter
1/4 cup all purpose flour
2 1/2 cups whole milk
2 tsp. salt
1/8 tsp. black pepper
1 tbs. prepared horseradish
1 tsp. yellow prepared mustard
8 oz. pkg. egg noodles, cooked
2 1/2 cups cooked corn beef, cubed
2 cups green peas, cooked
1 tbs. chopped red bell pepper

In a sauce pan over medium heat, add the butter. When the butter melts, stir in the all purpose flour. Stir constantly and cook for 1 minute. Add the milk, salt, black pepper, horseradish and mustard. Stir constantly and cook until the sauce thickens and bubbles. Remove the pan from the heat.

Preheat the oven to 350°. Spray a 2 quart casserole dish with non stick cooking spray. Add the noodles and half of the sauce to the casserole dish. Stir until the noodles are coated in the sauce.

Add the corn beef and green peas to the remaining sauce. Stir until combined and pour over the top of the noodles. Sprinkle the red bell pepper over the top. Bake for 20 minutes or until the casserole is hot and bubbly. Remove the casserole from the oven and serve.

You can substitute leftover steak or brisket for the corned beef if desired.

Ground Beef Artichoke Casserole

Makes 4 servings

12 oz. ground beef
1/2 cup sliced mushrooms
1/4 cup chopped onion
1 garlic clove, minced
14 oz. can artichoke hearts, drained and chopped
1/2 cup dry breadcrumbs
1/4 cup grated Parmesan cheese
1 tsp. dried rosemary
1/2 tsp. dried marjoram
Salt and black pepper to taste
3 eggs whites, stiffly beaten

In a skillet over medium heat, add the ground beef, mushrooms, onion and garlic. Stir frequently to break the ground beef into crumbles as it cooks. Cook for 8 minutes or until the ground beef is well browned and no longer pink. Remove the skillet from the heat and drain off any excess grease.

Add the artichokes, breadcrumbs, Parmesan cheese, rosemary, marjoram and salt and black pepper to taste to the skillet. Stir until well combined. Gently fold in the stiffly beaten egg whites.

Preheat the oven to 400°. Spoon the filling into a 1 quart casserole dish. Bake for 20 minutes or until the casserole is lightly browned. Remove the dish from the oven and serve.

2 CHICKEN & TURKEY

It never fails when I cook chicken, that I always have leftovers. I keep cooked chicken or turkey in the refrigerator all the time. They are easy to cook in the slow cooker and ready to toss into salads, casseroles or make sandwiches.

Avocado Chicken Casserole

Makes 6 servings

1/4 cup unsalted butter
1/4 cup all purpose flour
1/2 tsp. salt
1/4 tsp. garlic powder
1/4 tsp. onion powder
1/4 tsp. dried basil
1/4 tsp. dried marjoram
1/4 tsp. dried thyme
1 1/2 cups whole milk
1 cup half and half
6 cups hot cooked egg noodles
3 avocados, peeled and sliced
3 cups cubed cooked chicken
2 cups shredded cheddar cheese

In a sauce pan over medium heat, add the butter. When the butter melts, stir in the all purpose flour, salt, garlic powder, onion powder, basil, marjoram and thyme. Stir constantly and cook for 1 minute. Add the milk and half and half to the pan. Stir constantly and cook until the sauce thickens and bubbles. Remove the pan from the heat.

Preheat the oven to 350°. Spray a 9 x 13 casserole dish with non stick cooking spray. Spread half the noodles in the bottom of the casserole dish. Place half the avocados, chicken and cheddar cheese over the noodles. Pour half the sauce over the noodles. Repeat the layering process one more time using the remaining noodles, sauce, avocados, chicken and cheddar cheese.

Cover the dish with a lid or aluminum foil. Bake for 25 minutes or until the dish is hot and bubbly. Remove the dish from the oven and serve.

Chicken & Cornbread Casserole

Makes 6 servings

2 celery ribs, chopped
1/2 cup chopped onion
1 tbs. vegetable oil
3 cups crumbled cornbread
1 tbs. poultry seasoning
3 1/2 cups chopped cooked chicken
1 1/4 cups chicken broth
1 cup sour cream
1 egg, beaten
1 cup sliced cooked mushrooms
1/4 tsp. red pepper flakes
1/4 tsp. salt
2 tbs. melted unsalted butter
1 cup shredded sharp cheddar cheese

In a skillet over medium heat, add the celery, onion and vegetable oil. Saute the vegetables for 5 minutes or until the vegetables are tender. Remove the skillet from the heat. In a mixing bowl, add the cornbread and poultry seasoning. Toss until combined.

Spray a 11 x 7 casserole dish with non stick cooking spray. Preheat the oven to 350°. Spread half the cornbread in the bottom of the casserole dish. In a mixing bowl, add the onion and celery, chicken, chicken broth, sour cream, egg, mushrooms, red pepper flakes and salt. Stir until well combined. Spread the mixture over the top of the cornbread. Sprinkle the remaining cornbread over the top of the dish. Drizzle the butter over the cornbread.

Cover the dish with a lid or aluminum foil. Bake for 30 minutes or until the casserole is hot and bubbly. Remove the lid or aluminum foil from the dish. Sprinkle the cheddar cheese over the top of the dish. Bake for 10 minutes. Remove the dish from the oven and serve.

Tex Mex Chicken Squash Casserole

Makes 8 servings

10 oz. pkg. frozen chopped spinach, thawed
3 cups thinly sliced yellow squash
1 green bell pepper, cut into 1/2" pieces
1 cup thinly sliced onion
2 tbs. vegetable oil
3 cups shredded cooked chicken
12 corn tortillas, 6" size
10.75 oz. can cream of celery soup
1 cup sour cream
4 oz. can diced green chiles
1 envelope fajita seasoning mix
2 cups shredded sharp cheddar cheese

Drain the liquid from the spinach. Pat the spinach with paper towels and set aside. In a large skillet over medium heat, add the spinach, squash, green bell pepper, onion and vegetable oil. Saute the vegetables for 8 minutes or until they are tender. Remove the skillet from the heat and drain off any liquid.

Preheat the oven to 350°. Spray a 9 x 13 casserole dish with non stick cooking spray. Add the chicken to the skillet. Tear the corn tortillas into 1" pieces and add to the skillet. Add the cream of celery soup, sour cream, green chiles with liquid, fajita seasoning mix and 1 1/2 cups cheddar cheese to the skillet. Stir until combined spoon into the casserole dish.

Bake for 30 minutes or until the casserole is hot and bubbly. Sprinkle 1/2 cup cheddar cheese over the top of the casserole. Bake for 5 minutes or until the cheese melts. Remove the casserole from the oven and serve.

Country Chicken Casserole

Makes a 9 x 13 casserole dish

2 cans cream of chicken soup, 10.75 oz. size
3/4 cup mayonnaise
1/2 cup whole milk
3 tbs. honey
2 tbs. Dijon mustard
4 cups cubed cooked chicken
29 oz. pkg. frozen hashbrowns
3 cups sliced frozen carrots

Spray a 9 x 13 casserole dish with non stick cooking spray. Preheat the oven to 350°. Add all the ingredients to the casserole dish. Stir until combined. Place a lid or aluminum foil over the dish. Bake for 45 minutes or until the carrots are tender and the casserole hot and bubbly. Remove the dish from the oven and serve.

Chicken Dumpling Casserole

Makes 6 servings

1/2 cup chopped onion
1/2 cup chopped celery
2 garlic cloves, minced
1/4 cup unsalted butter, cubed
1/2 cup all purpose flour
2 tsp. granulated sugar
1 tsp. salt
1 tsp. dried basil
1/2 tsp. black pepper
4 cups chicken broth
10 oz. pkg. frozen green peas
4 cups cubed cooked chicken
2 cups Bisquick
2 tsp. dried basil
2/3 cup whole milk

In a large sauce pan over medium heat, add the onion, celery, garlic and butter. Saute the vegetables for 5 minutes. Add the all purpose flour, granulated sugar, salt, basil and black pepper to the pan. Stir constantly and cook for 2 minutes. Add the chicken broth to the pan. Stir constantly and cook for 2 minutes. Reduce the heat to low.

Add the green peas to the pan. Stir constantly and cook for 5 minutes. Remove the pan from the heat and stir in the chicken. Spray a 9 x 13 casserole dish with non stick cooking spray. Preheat the oven to 350°. Spoon the filling into the casserole dish.

In a mixing bowl, add the Bisquick, basil and milk. Stir until combined and a soft dough forms. Drop the dough, by tablespoonfuls, on the filling. Bake for 30 minutes. Cover the dish with a lid or aluminum foil. Bake for 10 minutes or until the dumplings are tender and done. Remove the dish from the oven and serve.

Smoked Sausage Chicken Rice Casserole

Makes 6 servings

4 tbs. unsalted butter
4 boneless skinless chicken breast, 4 oz. each
1 1/2 cups dry instant rice
6 oz. smoked sausage, cut into 1/2" slices
10.75 oz. can cream of chicken soup
10.75 oz. can cream of celery soup
1 cup sliced mushrooms
3/4 cup water
1/2 cup chicken broth
1 cup crushed cheese crackers
1 cup shredded cheddar cheese

In a skillet over medium heat, add 2 tablespoons butter. When the butter melts, add the chicken breast. Cook for 3 minutes on each side or until the chicken is no longer pink. Remove the skillet from the heat. Cut the chicken into bite size pieces.

Preheat the oven to 350°. Place the rice in the bottom of a 3 quart casserole dish. Place the chicken and smoked sausage over the rice. In a mixing bowl, add the cream of chicken soup, cream of celery soup, mushrooms, water and chicken broth. Stir until combined and pour over the top of the dish. Do not stir. Cover the dish with a lid or aluminum foil. Bake for 45 minutes or until the rice is tender and the casserole hot and bubbly. Remove the lid or aluminum foil from the dish.

Sprinkle the cheese crackers and cheddar cheese over the top of the casserole. Cut 2 tablespoons butter into small pieces and place over the crackers and cheese. Turn the oven to the broiler position. Broil for 5 minutes. Remove the dish from the oven and serve.

Mushroom Chicken Bake

Makes 8 servings

8 boneless skinless chicken breast, 4 oz. each
8 slices Swiss cheese, 1 oz. each
1 1/4 cups sliced fresh mushrooms
10.75 oz. can cream of mushroom soup
1/4 cup chicken broth
2 cups seasoned stuffing mix
1/4 cup melted unsalted butter

Preheat the oven to 350°. Spray a 9 x 13 casserole dish with non stick cooking spray. Place the chicken breast in the casserole dish. Place a Swiss cheese slice over each chicken breast. Sprinkle the mushrooms over the cheese.

In a mixing bowl, add the cream of mushroom soup and chicken broth. Stir until combined and pour over the chicken. Sprinkle the stuffing mix over the top of the chicken. Drizzle the butter over the stuffing mix.

Bake for 35 minutes or until the chicken breast are no longer pink and tender. Remove the casserole from the oven and serve.

Golden Chicken Casserole

Makes a 9 x 13 casserole dish

4 lbs. meaty chicken pieces (breast, thigh, leg)
1 large onion, quartered
3 tsp. salt
1/2 cup plus 1 tbs. unsalted butter
1/2 cup all purpose flour
1 cup evaporated whole milk
1/8 tsp. black pepper
1/2 tsp. ground turmeric
1/2 tsp. dried oregano
1 cup uncooked rice
2 1/2 cups boiling water
2 cups cooked mushrooms
1/2 cup chopped green onions
1/2 cup shredded cheddar cheese

In a large pot, add the chicken pieces, onion and 1 1/2 teaspoons salt. Cover the chicken with water and place the pot over medium heat. Cook the chicken for 1 1/2 hours or until the chicken is tender. Remove the pot from the heat. Remove the chicken from the pot but save the broth. You need 4 cups broth to make the sauce. If you do not have 4 cups broth, add water to make 4 cups. Cool the chicken until you can remove the meat from the bone. Chop the chicken into bite size pieces.

In a large sauce pan over medium heat, add 1/2 cup butter. When the butter melts, stir in the all purpose flour. Stir constantly and cook for 1 minute. Add 1 1/2 teaspoons salt, 4 cups chicken broth, evaporated milk, black pepper, turmeric and oregano. Continue to stir and cook until the sauce thickens and bubbles.

While the chicken is cooking, prepare the rice. Spray a 1 1/2 quart shallow casserole dish with non stick cooking spray. Place the rice in the casserole dish and add the boiling water and 1 tablespoon butter. Cover the dish with a lid or aluminum foil. Preheat the oven to 400°. Bake the rice for 30 minutes or until the rice is tender. Remove the dish from the oven.

Spray a 9 x 13 casserole dish with non stick cooking spray. Spread the rice in the bottom of the casserole dish. Place the chicken over the rice. Spread the mushrooms and green onions over the chicken. Pour the sauce over the top of the casserole. Sprinkle the cheddar cheese over the top.

Preheat the oven to 350°. Bake for 30 minutes or until the cheese is melted and the casserole hot and bubbly. Remove the casserole from the oven and serve.

Chili Chicken Enchilada Casserole

Makes 8 servings

2 cups diced cooked chicken
3 cups shredded Colby Jack cheese
4 oz. can diced green chiles, drained
3/4 cup sour cream
8 flour tortillas, 8" size
16 oz. can refried beans
10 oz. can red enchilada sauce
1/4 cup diced green onion
1 cup shredded lettuce
1 tomato, chopped

Preheat the oven to 350°. Spray a 9 x 13 casserole dish with non stick cooking spray. In a mixing bowl, add the chicken, Colby Jack cheese, green chiles and sour cream. Stir until well combined.

Place 3 tortillas in the bottom of the casserole dish. The tortillas will extend up the sides of the dish. Cut the tortillas to fit if needed. Spread half the refried beans over the tortillas. Spread half the chicken mixture over the beans. Spread half the enchilada sauce over the top. Place 3 tortillas over the top of the casserole. Spread the remaining refried beans over the tortillas. Spread the remaining chicken mixture over the beans. Place 2 tortillas over the top of the casserole. Spread the remaining enchilada sauce over the tortillas.

Cover the dish with a lid or aluminum foil. Bake for 45 minutes or until the casserole is hot and bubbly. Remove the dish from the oven. Sprinkle the green onion, lettuce and tomato over the top and serve.

Tortilla Chicken Casserole

Makes 8 servings

3 tbs. vegetable oil
1 1/2 cups minced red bell pepper
1 1/2 cups minced onion
2 tbs. minced garlic
1/2 tsp. salt
2 1/2 tsp. ground cumin
1/4 cup all purpose flour
1 1/2 cups chicken broth
1 cup sour cream
5 cups chopped cooked chicken
12 corn tortillas, 6" size
3 cups shredded Monterey Jack cheese

In a large skillet over medium heat, add the vegetable oil. When the oil is hot, add the red bell pepper, onion and garlic. Saute the vegetables for 10 minutes or until they are soft. Add the salt and cumin to the skillet. Saute for 1 minute. Add the all purpose flour, chicken broth and sour cream to the skillet. Stir constantly and cook for 5 minutes.

Add the chicken to the skillet and stir until combined. Remove the skillet from the heat. Wrap the corn tortillas in a damp paper towel. Microwave for 20 seconds or until the tortillas soften. Remove the tortillas from the microwave.

Preheat the oven to 350°. Spray a 9 x 13 casserole dish with non stick cooking spray. Place 4 corn tortillas in the casserole dish. Spread 1/3 of the chicken filling over the tortillas. Sprinkle 1 cup Monterey Jack cheese over the filling. Repeat the layering process 2 more times. Bake for 35 minutes or until the casserole is hot and bubbly. Remove the dish from the oven and cool for 5 minutes before serving.

You can cover the casserole dish and refrigerate the unbaked casserole up to 24 hours before serving.

Chicken Cordon Bleu Casserole

Makes 8 servings

2 boxes instant long grain & wild rice mix, 6 oz. size
4 cups water
4 oz. cooked ham, cut into thin strips
1 1/2 lbs. chicken breast tenderloins
16 oz. jar Alfredo sauce
1/2 tsp. paprika
1 cup shredded Swiss cheese
1 tbs. chopped fresh parsley

Preheat the oven to 350°. Spray a 9 x 13 casserole dish with non stick cooking spray. Add the rice mix with seasoning packets and water to the casserole dish. Stir until well combined. Place the ham over the rice. Place the chicken tenderloins over the ham. Spread the alfredo sauce over the chicken. Sprinkle the paprika over the chicken.

Cover the dish with a lid or aluminum foil. Bake for 40 minutes. Remove the lid or aluminum foil and cook until the rice is tender. Sprinkle the Swiss cheese over the top of the casserole. Bake for 10 minutes. Remove the casserole from the oven and sprinkle the parsley over the top before serving.

Alfredo Chicken Bake

Makes 4 servings

2 cups cooked chicken breast, diced
1/2 cup frozen green peas
1/2 cup shredded Swiss cheese
3/4 cup jarred or refrigerated Alfredo pasta sauce
2 tbs. slivered almonds
1 cup Bisquick
1/3 cup whole milk

Preheat the oven to 425°. Spray a sauce pan with non stick cooking spray. Add the chicken, green peas, Swiss cheese, alfredo sauce and almonds to the pan. Stir constantly and cook until the filling is hot and bubbly. Remove the pan from the heat and spoon the casserole into a 1 1/2 quart casserole dish.

In a small bowl, whisk together the Bisquick and milk. Stir until a soft dough forms. Drop the dough, by tablespoonfuls, onto the hot filling. Bake for 20 minutes or until the dumplings are golden brown and the casserole bubbly. Remove the dish from the oven and serve.

Creamy Chicken, Spinach & Pasta Casserole

Makes 8 servings

1 tbs. olive oil
1/4 cup chopped onion
1/4 cup chopped red bell pepper
2 boneless skinless chicken breast, 6 oz. each
10 oz. pkg. frozen spinach, thawed and drained
4 oz. can sliced mushrooms
2 cups shredded Swiss cheese
1 cup sour cream
3/4 cup half and half
2 eggs, beaten
1/2 tsp. salt
4 cups cooked egg noodles

In a large skillet over medium heat, add the olive oil, onion and red bell pepper. Saute the vegetables for 5 minutes or until the vegetables are tender. Cut the chicken into 1" pieces. Add the spinach, chicken and mushrooms to the skillet. Stir until combined. Remove the skillet from the heat.

In a mixing bowl, add the Swiss cheese, sour cream, half and half, eggs and salt. Whisk until combined. Add the noodles to the skillet and toss until all the ingredients are combined.

Preheat the oven to 350°. Spray a 9 x 13 casserole dish with non stick cooking spray. Spoon the casserole into the dish. Bake for 35 minutes or until the casserole is hot and bubbly. Remove the dish from the oven and serve.

Southern Chicken & Rice Casserole

Makes a 9 x 13 casserole dish

1 quart water
2 tsp. salt
4 lbs. meaty chicken pieces (breast, thigh, leg)
2 tbs. all purpose flour
1/2 tsp. garlic salt
1/8 tsp. black pepper
1/2 cup half and half
1 cup shredded cheddar cheese
4 cups cooked rice
1 cup cooked sliced mushrooms
1 tbs. fresh chopped parsley
4 slices bacon, cooked and crumbled
1/4 cup cracker crumbs
1/4 tsp. poultry seasoning

In a large pot over medium heat, add the water, salt and chicken. Cook the chicken for 1 1/2 hours or until the chicken is tender. Remove the pot from the heat. Remove the chicken from the pot but save the broth. You need 2 cups broth for this recipe. You can use 2 cups canned chicken broth if desired. Cool the chicken until you can remove the meat from the bone. Chop the chicken into bite size pieces.

In a sauce pan over medium heat, add the chicken broth, all purpose flour, garlic salt, black pepper and half and half. Whisk constantly until the liquids are smooth and combined. Stir constantly and cook until the sauce thickens and bubbles. Remove the pan from the heat and stir in the cheddar cheese.

Preheat the oven to 450°. Spray a 9 x 13 casserole dish with non stick cooking spray. In a large mixing bowl, add the rice, chicken, mushrooms and parsley to the dish. Stir until combined. Place half the rice mixture in the bottom of the casserole dish. Spread half of the sauce over the mixture. Place the remaining rice mixture over the sauce and spread the remaining sauce over rice mixture.

In a small bowl, add the bacon, cracker crumbs and poultry seasoning. Stir until combined and sprinkle over the top of the casserole. Bake for 30 minutes or until the casserole is bubbly and the topping golden brown. Remove the casserole from the oven and serve.

Chicken Pot Pie Casserole

Makes 4 servings

4 1/2 cups frozen hashbrowns
2 cups frozen cut green beans
1 cup frozen sliced carrots
4 boneless skinless chicken breast, 6 oz. each
10.75 oz. can cream of mushroom soup
3/4 cup water
2 tbs. dry onion soup mix

Spray a 9 x 13 casserole dish with non stick cooking spray. Preheat the oven to 350°. Add the hashbrowns, green beans and carrots to the casserole dish. Stir until combined. Place the chicken breast over the top of the casserole.

In a mixing bowl, add the cream of mushroom soup, water and onion soup mix. Stir until combined and pour over the top of the casserole. Cover the dish with a lid or aluminum foil. Bake for 30 minutes or until the chicken is no longer pink and tender. The vegetables should be tender when ready. Remove the dish from the oven and serve.

Chicken Green Bean Casserole

Makes 6 servings

6 tbs. unsalted butter
6 tbs. all purpose flour
1 1/2 cups chicken broth
1/2 cup whole milk
1 tsp. soy sauce
1/2 tsp. salt
1/8 tsp. black pepper
2/3 cup grated Parmesan cheese
8 cups cooked green beans
3 cups cubed cooked chicken

In a large sauce pan over medium heat, add the butter. When the butter melts, stir in the all purpose flour. Stir constantly and cook for 1 minute. Add the chicken broth, milk, soy sauce, salt and black pepper. Stir constantly and cook until the sauce thickens and bubbles. Remove the pan from the heat and stir in 1/3 cup Parmesan cheese, green beans and chicken.

Preheat the oven to 375°. Spoon the casserole into a 2 quart casserole dish. Sprinkle 1/3 cup Parmesan cheese over the top of the casserole. Bake for 15 minutes or until the casserole is hot and bubbly. Remove the dish from the oven and serve.

Onion Topped Turkey Divan Casserole

Makes 4 servings

16 oz. pkg. frozen broccoli florets, thawed
2 cups cooked diced turkey
10.75 oz. can cream of chicken soup
1/2 cup mayonnaise
1/2 cup whole milk
1 cup shredded cheddar cheese
1 cup French fried onions

Preheat the oven to 350°. Spray a 2 quart casserole dish with non stick cooking spray. Add the broccoli and turkey to the dish. In a mixing bowl, add the cream of chicken soup, mayonnaise, milk and cheddar cheese. Stir until combined and spread over the top of the casserole.

Place a lid or aluminum foil on the casserole dish. Bake for 30 minutes. Remove the lid or aluminum foil from the dish. Sprinkle the French fried onions over the top of the casserole. Bake for 20 minutes or until the casserole is hot and bubbly. Remove the casserole from the oven and serve.

Turkey Wild Rice Casserole

Makes 8 servings

1/4 cup unsalted butter
1 cup chopped onion
1 1/4 lbs. ground turkey
1/4 tsp. black pepper
3 cups cooked wild rice
2 cups shredded cheddar cheese
10.75 oz. can cream of chicken soup
1 cup sour cream
4 cups chunky hashbrowns
1/3 cup breadcrumbs

In a skillet over medium heat, add the butter, onion and ground turkey. Stir frequently to break the turkey into crumbles as it cooks. Cook for 5 minutes or until the turkey is well browned and no longer pink. Remove the skillet from the heat. Stir in the black pepper, wild rice, cheddar cheese, cream of chicken soup and sour cream.

Spread the hashbrowns in the bottom of a 9 x 13 casserole dish. Spread the turkey mixture over the hashbrowns. Sprinkle the breadcrumbs over the top of the dish. Bake for 40 minutes or until the hashbrowns are tender and the casserole hot and bubbly. Remove the dish from the oven and serve.

Turkey & Ham Spaghetti Casserole

Makes 4 servings

12 cups water
7 oz. pkg. spaghetti noodles, broken into 2" pieces
2 cups chopped cooked turkey
3/4 cup diced cooked ham
1/4 cup minced red bell pepper
1/4 cup minced green bell pepper
10.75 oz. can cream of mushroom soup
1/2 cup chicken broth
1/8 tsp. celery salt
1/8 tsp. black pepper
1 1/2 cups shredded cheddar cheese

In a dutch oven over medium heat, add 12 cups water. When the water is boiling, add the spaghetti noodles. Cook for 7 minutes or until the noodles are tender. Remove the pan from the heat and drain all the water from the noodles.

Add the turkey, ham, red bell pepper, green bell pepper, cream of mushroom soup, chicken broth, celery salt and black pepper to the spaghetti noodles. Stir until combined. Place the pan back on the stove and cook until all the ingredients are thoroughly heated. Remove the pan from the heat and stir in 1 cup cheddar cheese.

Preheat the oven to 350°. Spray an 8" square baking pan with non stick cooking spray. Spoon the casserole into the pan. Sprinkle 1/2 cup cheddar cheese over the top of the casserole. Bake for 20 minutes or until the casserole is hot and bubbly. Remove the dish from the oven and serve.

Cheesy Turkey Spaghetti Casserole

Makes 8 servings

1 lb. ground turkey
1 tbs. vegetable oil
15 oz. can mixed vegetables, drained
10.75 oz. can cream of chicken soup
10.75 oz. can cream of mushroom soup
1 cup whole milk
1/4 cup chicken broth
6 cups cooked linguine noodles
1 cup sliced mushrooms
3/4 cup grated Parmesan cheese

In a large skillet over medium heat, add the turkey and vegetable oil. Stir frequently and cook for 8 minutes or until the turkey is no longer pink and well browned. Remove the skillet from the heat.

Add the mixed vegetables, cream of chicken soup, cream of mushroom soup, milk and chicken broth to the skillet. Stir until well combined. Stir in the linguine noodles, mushrooms and 1/2 cup Parmesan cheese. Stir until combined and spoon into an 9 x 13 casserole dish.

Preheat the oven to 400°. Sprinkle 1/4 cup Parmesan cheese over the top of the dish. Bake for 30 minutes or until the casserole is hot and bubbly. Remove the dish from the oven and serve.

Homestyle Turkey Biscuit Casserole

Makes 4 servings

10.75 oz. can cream of celery soup
1/2 cup whole milk
2 cups frozen mixed vegetables
2 cups cubed cooked turkey
1 cup chive and onion sour cream
1/4 tsp. poultry seasoning
4 frozen biscuits

Preheat the oven to 375°. Spray an 8" square baking pan with non stick cooking spray. In a sauce pan over medium heat, add the cream of celery soup, milk, mixed vegetables, turkey, sour cream and poultry seasoning. Stir constantly and bring the filling to a boil. Remove the pan from the heat.

Spoon the filling into the baking pan. Place the biscuits over the filling. Bake for 30 minutes or until the biscuits are golden brown. Remove the casserole from the oven and serve.

Green Bean and Turkey Casserole

Makes 6 servings

2 cups cooked chopped turkey
2 cups frozen green beans
10.75 oz. can cream of mushroom soup
1 cup whole milk
1 cup shredded cheddar cheese
1 3/4 cups water
3 tbs. unsalted butter
1/2 tsp. salt
2 cups dry mashed potato flakes
1/2 cup french fried onions

In a sauce pan over medium heat, add the turkey, green beans, cream of mushroom soup and 1/3 cup milk. Stir constantly and cook for 6 minutes. The filling should be bubbly when ready. Add the cheddar cheese and stir until combined.

In a sauce pan over medium heat, add 2/3 cup milk, water, butter and salt. Bring the water to a boil and remove the pan from the heat. Stir in the potato flakes. Stir until smooth and combined.

Preheat the oven to 375°. Spoon the turkey filling into a 2 quart casserole dish. Spread the mashed potatoes over the top. Bake for 10 minutes. Sprinkle the fried onions over the top. Bake for 10 minutes or until the casserole is hot and bubbly and the fried onions golden brown. Remove the dish from the oven and serve.

Leftover Thanksgiving Turkey Dinner Bake

Makes 6 servings

2 1/2 cups chopped cooked turkey
2 1/2 cups cooked cornbread dressing
1 1/2 cups turkey gravy
3 cups prepared mashed potatoes
1/2 tbs. unsalted butter

Preheat the oven to 325°. Spray an 8" square baking pan with non stick cooking spray. Place the turkey in the baking pan. Spread the cornbread dressing over the turkey. Spread the gravy over the dressing. Spread the mashed potatoes over the gravy. Cut the butter into small pieces and place over the potatoes.

Bake for 45 minutes. Remove the casserole from the oven and cool the casserole for 10 minutes before serving.

Spiced Turkey, Squash and Apple Casserole

Makes 4 servings

4 skinless turkey thighs, 6 oz. each
1 lb. acorn squash, cut into 1" rings
4 cored apples, cut into 1/2" rings
1/4 cup apple juice
3 tbs. light brown sugar
1/2 tsp. ground cinnamon
1/4 tsp. ground nutmeg

Preheat the oven to 350°. Place the turkey thighs in a 9 x 13 baking dish. Place the squash and apple rings over the turkey thighs. In a small bowl, add the apple juice, brown sugar, cinnamon and nutmeg. Stir until combined and pour over the top of the dish.

Cover the dish with a lid or aluminum foil. Bake for 1 hour. Remove the lid or aluminum foil. Spoon the pan juices over the turkey, squash and apple. Bake for 15 minutes or until the turkey is no longer pink and reaches an internal temperature of at least 180° on a meat thermometer. Remove the dish from the oven and cool for 5 minutes before serving.

Turkey Taco Casserole

Makes 4 servings

2 cups crumbled corn chips
16 oz. can refried beans
2 cups shredded Monterey Jack cheese
1 cup salsa
2 cups shredded cooked turkey
1 tsp. taco seasoning
1 green onion, sliced
1 tomato, chopped

Spray a 2 1/2 quart casserole dish with non stick cooking spray. Place the corn chips in the casserole dish. Add the refried beans to a microwavable bowl. Microwave for 1 minute or until the beans are thoroughly heated. Remove the bowl from the microwave and stir in 1 cup Monterey Jack cheese and the salsa. Stir until combined and spread over the corn chips.

In a small bowl, stir together the turkey and taco seasoning. Sprinkle the turkey over the beans. Sprinkle 1 cup Monterey Jack cheese over the turkey. Preheat the oven to 400°. Bake for 25 minutes. Remove the dish from the oven and sprinkle the green onion and tomato over the dish.

Turkey Cazuela Casserole

Makes 6 servings

4 cups cooked pasta
1 1/3 cups fried onions
2 cups cubed cooked turkey
10.75 oz. can cream of chicken soup
1 cup picante sauce
1/2 cup sour cream
1 cup shredded cheddar cheese

Preheat the oven to 350°. Spray a 2 quart casserole dish with non stick cooking spray. Place the pasta in the bottom of the dish. Sprinkle the fried onions over the pasta. Sprinkle the turkey over the pasta.

In a mixing bowl, add the cream of chicken soup, picante sauce and sour cream. Stir until combined and spread over the pasta. Cover the dish with a lid or aluminum foil. Bake for 40 minutes. Remove the lid or aluminum foil from the dish.

Sprinkle the cheddar cheese over the casserole. Bake for 5 minutes or until the cheese is melted and the casserole hot and bubbly. Remove the dish from the oven and serve.

Southwest Turkey Casserole

Makes 4 servings

6 cups water
1 cup dry elbow macaroni
1/2 cup chopped onion
1/2 cup chopped red bell pepper
9 tsp. unsalted butter
2 tbs. vegetable oil
2 tbs. all purpose flour
1 tsp. salt
1 tsp. ground cumin
1/8 tsp. black pepper
2 cups whole milk
2 cups shredded cheddar cheese
2 cups cubed cooked turkey
10 oz. can diced tomatoes with green chiles
2/3 cup frozen whole kernel corn
2/3 cup frozen green peas

In a sauce pan over medium heat, add the water. When the water is boiling, add the elbow macaroni. Cook for 6 minutes or until the macaroni is tender. Remove the pan from the heat and drain all the water from the macaroni.

In a large skillet over medium heat, add the onion, red bell pepper, butter and vegetable oil. Saute the vegetables for 5 minutes. Add the all purpose flour, salt, cumin and black pepper. Stir constantly and cook for 2 minutes. Add the milk to the skillet. Stir constantly and cook for 2 minutes or until the sauce thickens and bubbles. Remove the skillet from the heat and stir in the cheddar cheese. Stir until until the cheese melts.

Add the elbow macaroni, turkey, tomatoes with liquid, corn and green peas to the skillet. Stir until combined. Preheat the oven to 350°. Spray a 2 quart casserole dish with non stick cooking spray. Spoon the casserole into the dish. Bake for 25 minutes or until the casserole is hot and bubbly. Remove the dish from the oven and serve.

3 HAM & SAUSAGES

Ham is always great in a casserole and cooked ham is so easy to buy at the store. I always keep ham in the refrigerator for casseroles. Smoked sausages and Italian sausages are delicious in casseroles. I keep them on hand not only for sandwiches but for quick and easy meals.

Pasta and Ham Bake

Makes 4 servings

2 quarts water
2 1/2 tsp. salt
1 tbs. vegetable oil
1 3/4 cups elbow macaroni
2 cups diced cooked ham
1 1/2 cups shredded cheddar cheese
2 tbs. unsalted butter
1/4 cup all purpose flour
1/4 tsp. dry mustard
2 1/2 cups whole milk
1/2 cup crushed potato chips

In a large sauce pan over medium heat, add the water, 2 teaspoons salt and vegetable oil. When the water is boiling, add the elbow macaroni. Cook for 6 minutes or until the macaroni is tender. Remove the pan from the heat and drain all the water from the macaroni.

In a mixing bowl, add the macaroni, ham and 1 cup cheddar cheese. In a sauce pan over medium heat, add the butter. When the butter melts, stir in the all purpose flour. Stir constantly and cook for 1 minute. Add the dry mustard, 1/2 teaspoon salt and milk to the pan. Stir constantly and cook until the sauce thickens and bubbles. Remove the pan from the heat and add to the mixing bowl with the macaroni. Stir until all the ingredients are combined.

Preheat the oven to 350°. Spoon the casserole into a 2 quart casserole dish. Sprinkle the potato chips and 1/2 cup cheddar cheese over the top of the casserole. Bake for 25 minutes. Remove the dish from the oven and serve.

Ham and Vegetable Cobbler

Makes 6 servings

1/4 cup unsalted butter
1/4 cup all purpose flour
3 1/2 cups whole milk
1/2 tsp. dried thyme
1 tsp. chicken bouillon granules
2 cups diced cooked ham
10 oz. pkg. frozen green peas
4 oz. jar sliced mushrooms
1 cup thinly sliced carrots
9" refrigerated crust

In a large sauce pan over medium heat, add the butter. When the butter melts, stir in the all purpose flour. Stir constantly and cook for 1 minute. Add the milk, thyme and chicken bouillon to the pan. Stir constantly and cook until the sauce thickens and bubbles.

Add the ham, green peas, mushrooms and carrots. Stir constantly and cook for 5 minutes. Remove the pan from the heat. Preheat the oven to 450°. Spray a 11 x 7 casserole dish with non stick cooking spray. Spoon the ham and vegetables into the casserole dish.

Remove the pie crust from the package. Cut the pie crust into 1 1/2" wide strips. Place the strips over the filling forming a lattice crust. Bake for 40 minutes or until the pie crust is golden brown and the vegetables tender. Remove the dish from the oven and serve.

Creamy Ham & Vegetable Casserole

Makes 6 servings

3 cups cauliflower florets
4 tbs. unsalted butter
1/3 cup all purpose flour
1 cup whole milk
1 cup shredded cheddar cheese
1/2 cup sour cream
2 cups cubed cooked ham
1 cup cooked sliced mushrooms
1 cup soft breadcrumbs
1 tbs. cold butter, cut into small pieces

In a sauce pan over medium heat, add the cauliflower. Cover the cauliflower with water and cook for 10 minutes. The cauliflower should be tender when ready. Remove the pan from the heat and drain all the water from the cauliflower.

In a sauce pan over medium heat, add 4 tablespoons butter. When the butter melts, add the all purpose flour. Stir constantly and cook for 2 minutes. Add the milk and stir until the sauce thickens and bubbles. Stir in the cheddar cheese and sour cream. Remove the pan from the heat.

Add the cauliflower, ham and mushrooms to the sauce. Stir until combined. Preheat the oven to 350°. Spoon the filling into a 2 quart casserole dish. Sprinkle the breadcrumbs over the top of the casserole. Place 1 tablespoon cold butter pieces over the breadcrumbs. Bake for 45 minutes. Remove the casserole from the oven and serve.

Asparagus Ham Casserole

Makes 6 servings

10 oz. pkg. frozen asparagus cuts
4 hard boiled eggs, peeled and chopped
1 cup cubed cooked ham
2 tbs. quick cooking tapioca
1/4 cup shredded Velveeta cheese
2 tbs. chopped green bell pepper
2 tbs. chopped onion
1 tbs. minced fresh parsley
1 tbs. lemon juice
1/2 cup half and half
1 cup condensed cream of mushroom soup
1 cup soft bread crumbs
2 tbs. melted unsalted butter

In a large sauce pan over medium heat, add the asparagus. Cover the asparagus with water and bring the asparagus to a boil. Cook for 3 minutes. Remove the pan from the heat and drain all the water from the asparagus. Pat the asparagus dry with a paper towel.

Preheat the oven to 375°. In a 2 1/2 quart casserole dish, add the asparagus, eggs, ham, tapioca, Velveeta cheese, green bell pepper, onion, parsley, lemon juice, half and half and cream of mushroom soup. Stir until combined.

In a small bowl, stir together the breadcrumbs and butter. Sprinkle the breadcrumbs over the top of the casserole. Bake for 30 minutes or until the casserole is hot and bubbly. Remove the dish from the oven and cool for 5 minutes before serving.

Au Gratin Ham and Potato Casserole

Makes 8 servings

3 tbs. unsalted butter
3 tbs. all purpose flour
2 cups whole milk
1 1/2 cups shredded cheddar cheese
1 tbs. Dijon mustard
2 cups cooked ham, cut into thin strips
24 oz. pkg. frozen shredded hashbrowns
10 oz. pkg. frozen chopped spinach, thawed

In a sauce pan over medium heat, add the butter. When the butter melts, stir in the all purpose flour. Stir constantly and cook for 1 minute. Add the whole milk to the pan. Stir constantly and cook until the sauce thickens and bubbles. Stir in the cheddar cheese and Dijon mustard. Cook until the cheese melts. Remove the dish from the heat.

Preheat the oven to 350°. Place half the ham in a 3 quart casserole dish. Spread half the hashbrowns over the ham. Spread half the cheese sauce over the hashbrowns. Spread the spinach over the hashbrowns. Spread the remaining ham and hashbrowns over the spinach. Spread the remaining cheese sauce over the top of the dish.

Bake for 30 minutes or until the dish is hot and bubbly. Remove the dish from the oven and serve.

Cheesy Ham Broccoli Bake

Makes 6 servings

3 cups dry egg noodles
16 oz. pkg. frozen broccoli spears
2 cups diced cooked ham
2 cups shredded American cheese
1 cup whole milk
1/4 tsp. black pepper
1 cup sliced cooked mushrooms
3/4 cup crushed cheese crackers

In a large sauce pan over medium heat, add the noodles and broccoli. Cover the noodles with water and bring the noodles to boil. Cook for 6 minutes or until the noodles and broccoli are tender. Remove the pan from the heat and drain all the water from the noodles and broccoli.

Ad the ham, American cheese, milk, black pepper and mushrooms to the noodles. Stir until all the ingredients are combined. Preheat the oven to 350°. Spray a 2 quart casserole dish with non stick cooking spray. Spoon the noodles and vegetables into the casserole dish.

Sprinkle the cheese crackers over the top of the casserole. Bake for 20 minutes or until the dish is hot and bubbly. Remove the casserole from the oven and serve.

Ham and Potato Brunch Casserole

Makes 6 servings

8 oz. Velveeta cheese, melted
3/4 cup whole milk
4 cups diced potatoes
2 cups diced cooked ham
16 oz. bag frozen mixed vegetables, thawed
1/2 cup chopped onion
1 cup shredded Monterey Jack cheese
1 cup butter cracker crumbs

Preheat the oven to 350°. Spray a 3 quart casserole dish with non stick cooking spray. In a mixing bowl, add the Velveeta cheese, milk, potatoes, ham, mixed vegetables and onion. Stir until combined and spoon into the casserole dish. Cover the dish with a lid or aluminum foil.

Bake for 45 minutes. Stir the casserole occasionally while cooking. Sprinkle the Monterey Jack cheese and cracker crumbs over the casserole. Bake for 10 minutes or until the cheese is melted and cracker crumbs toasted. Remove the casserole from the oven and serve.

Double Cheese Baked Casserole

You can leave the ham out of this dish and have a comforting meatless supper.

Makes 6 servings

2 cups hot cooked elbow macaroni
1/4 cup unsalted butter
1 cup soft breadcrumbs
1 cup shredded cheddar cheese
1/2 cup shredded Swiss cheese
1 cup finely chopped cooked ham
3 eggs, beaten
1 tbs. dried minced onion
1 tbs. minced fresh parsley
1/4 tsp. salt
1/8 tsp. black pepper
1 1/2 cups whole milk, heated
Paprika to taste

Preheat the oven to 325°. Spray a 2 quart casserole dish with non stick cooking spray. In a mixing bowl, add the elbow macaroni and butter. Toss until the butter melts and the macaroni is coated in the butter.

Add the breadcrumbs, cheddar cheese, Swiss cheese, ham, eggs, onion, parsley, salt, black pepper and milk to the bowl. Stir until well combined. Spoon the mixture into the casserole dish. Sprinkle paprika to taste over the top of the dish.

Bake for 40 minutes or until the casserole is hot and bubbly. Remove the dish from the oven and serve.

Ham Scrambled Egg Casserole

Makes a 9 x 13 casserole dish

1/2 cup plus 1 tbs. unsalted butter
7 1/2 tsp. all purpose flour
2 cups whole milk
1/2 tsp. salt
1/8 tsp. black pepper
1 cup shredded Velveeta cheese
1 cup cubed cooked ham
1/4 cup chopped green onion
12 beaten eggs
4 oz. jar sliced mushrooms, drained
2 1/4 cups soft breadcrumbs

In a sauce pan over medium heat, add 2 tablespoons butter and all purpose flour. Stir constantly and cook for 2 minutes. Add the whole milk, salt and black pepper to the pan. Stir constantly and cook until the sauce thickens and bubbles. Add the Velveeta cheese and stir until the cheese melts. Remove the pan from the heat.

In a large skillet over medium heat, add 3 tablespoons butter, ham and green onion. Saute the ham for 5 minutes. Add the beaten eggs and mushrooms to the skillet. Stir constantly and cook until the eggs are scrambled and set. Remove the skillet from the heat. Add the cheese sauce to the skillet and stir until combined.

Spray a 9 x 13 casserole dish with non stick cooking spray. Spread the eggs in the casserole dish. In a small bowl, toss together the remaining butter and breadcrumbs. Sprinkle the breadcrumbs over the top of the casserole. Cover the casserole with a lid or plastic wrap. Refrigerate the casserole for 8 hours.

Preheat the oven to 350°. Remove the lid or plastic wrap from the casserole. Bake for 30 minutes or until the dish is hot and bubbly. Remove the casserole from the oven and serve.

Spam Hashbrown Casserole

Makes 8 servings

32 oz. pkg. frozen hashbrowns, thawed
1/2 cup unsalted butter, melted
1 tsp. salt
1 tsp. black pepper
1/2 tsp. garlic powder
2 cups shredded cheddar cheese
12 oz. can Spam, cubed
10.75 oz. can cream of chicken soup
1 1/2 cups sour cream
1/2 cup whole milk
1/2 cup chopped onion
4 oz. can diced green chiles drained
2 cups crushed potato chips

Preheat the oven to 350°. Spray a 9 x 13 casserole dish with non stick cooking spray. In a large mixing bowl, add the hashbrowns, melted butter, salt, black pepper, garlic powder, cheddar cheese, Spam, cream of chicken soup, sour cream, whole milk, onion and green chiles. Stir until well combined. Spoon the casserole into the dish.

Sprinkle the potato chips over the top. Bake for 1 hour or until the hashbrowns are tender and the casserole hot, bubbly and golden brown. Remove the dish from the oven and cool for 5 minutes before serving.

You can use 2 cups diced cooked ham, turkey or chicken for the Spam if desired. For a beef version, use 2 cups diced cooked beef or ground beef instead of the Spam. Replace the cream of chicken soup with cream of mushroom soup if using the beef.

Sausage Sweet Potato Casserole

Makes 6 servings

4 cups tart peeled apples, thinly sliced
4 cups sweet potatoes, peeled and thinly sliced
2 tsp. dried minced onion
2 tsp. salt
1/2 cup maple syrup
1/2 cup apple juice
1/4 cup unsalted butter, melted
1 lb. ground pork sausage
1/3 cup dry breadcrumbs

Spray a 2 quart casserole dish with non stick cooking spray. Preheat the oven to 350°. Place the apples and sweet potatoes in the casserole dish. Sprinkle the onion and salt over the apples and sweet potatoes. Toss to combine the apples and sweet potatoes.

In a small bowl, add the maple syrup, apple juice and butter. Whisk until combined and pour over the apples and sweet potatoes. Cover the dish with a lid or aluminum foil. Bake for 45 minutes.

While the casserole is baking, add the sausage to a skillet. Place the skillet over medium heat. Stir the sausage frequently to break the sausage into crumbles as it cooks. Remove the skillet from the heat and drain off the excess grease. Sprinkle the breadcrumbs over the sausage and toss until combined.

Remove the casserole from the oven and remove the aluminum foil. Spread the sausage over the casserole. Bake for 20 minutes or until the apples and sweet potatoes are tender. Remove the dish from the oven and serve.

Sausage Macaroni & Cheese Bake

Makes 6 servings

1 lb. ground pork sausage
1 1/2 cups whole milk
12 oz. cheddar cheese, cubed
1/2 cup Dijon mustard
1 cup diced fresh tomatoes
1 cup sliced fresh mushrooms
1/3 cup sliced green onions
6 cups cooked elbow macaroni
2 tsp. grated Parmesan cheese

In a skillet over medium heat, add the sausage. Stir frequently to break the sausage into crumbles as it cooks. Cook for 8 minutes or until the sausage is well browned and no longer pink. Remove the skillet from the heat and drain all the excess grease from the sausage.

In a large sauce pan over low heat, add the whole milk, cheddar cheese and Dijon mustard. Stir constantly and cook until the cheese melts. Do not let the milk boil. Stir in the sausage, tomatoes, mushrooms, green onions and elbow macaroni. Stir until well combined and remove the pan from the heat.

Preheat the oven to 350°. Spray a 2 quart casserole dish with non stick cooking spray. Spoon the macaroni and cheese into the casserole dish. Bake for 20 minutes. Sprinkle the Parmesan cheese over the top. Bake for 5 minutes. Remove the dish from the oven and serve.

Sausage Eggplant Casserole

Makes 4 servings

1 eggplant, peeled and cut into 1" cubes
8 oz. ground pork sausage
1 onion, chopped
1 egg, beaten
1/2 cup dry breadcrumbs
1 tbs. unsalted butter, melted
1/4 cup cracker crumbs

Add the eggplant to a sauce pan over medium heat. Add water to cover the eggplant. Cook the eggplant about 10 minutes or until the eggplant is tender. Remove the pan from the heat and drain all the water from the eggplant.

In a small skillet over medium heat, add the sausage and onion. Stir frequently to break the sausage into crumbles as it cooks. Cook about 6 minutes or until the sausage is well browned and no longer pink. Remove the skillet from the heat and drain off all the excess grease.

Spray a 1 quart casserole dish with non stick cooking spray. Preheat the oven to 350°. Add the eggplant, sausage and onion, egg and breadcrumbs to the casserole dish. Stir until well combined. In a small bowl, stir together the butter and cracker crumbs. Sprinkle the cracker crumbs over the top of the casserole. Bake for 25 minutes. Remove the dish from the oven and serve.

Easy Lasagna Pizza Casserole

Makes 8 servings

1 lb. ground Italian sausage
12 oz. wide egg noodles, hot and cooked
4 1/2 cups pizza or spaghetti sauce
2 cups shredded cheddar cheese
2 cups shredded mozzarella cheese
6 oz. sliced pepperoni

In a skillet over medium heat, add the Italian sausage. Stir frequently to break the sausage into crumbles as it cooks. Cook for 8 minutes or until the sausage is well browned and no longer pink. Remove the skillet from the heat and drain all the excess grease from the skillet.

Spray a 9 x 13 casserole dish with non stick cooking spray. Preheat the oven to 350°. Spread half the egg noodles in the bottom of the dish. Sprinkle half the sausage over the noodles. Spread half the pizza sauce over the top of the dish. Sprinkle 1 cup cheddar cheese and 1 cup mozzarella cheese over the sauce. Place half the pepperoni slices over the cheeses. Repeat the layering process one more time using the remaining sausage, noodles, pizza sauce, cheddar cheese, mozzarella cheese and pepperoni.

Bake for 40 minutes or until the casserole is hot and bubbly. Remove the dish from the oven and cool for 5 minutes before serving.

Italian Sausage and Cheese Potato Casserole

Makes 6 servings

1 lb. ground Italian sausage
4 cups peeled potatoes, cubed
1 cup shredded Monterey Jack cheese
1/4 cup chopped green onion
4 oz. can diced green chiles, drained
6 eggs
3/4 cup whole milk
1/4 tsp. salt
1/8 tsp. black pepper
1/2 cup grated Parmesan cheese

In a skillet over medium heat, add the Italian sausage. Stir frequently to break the sausage into crumbles as it cooks. Cook for 8 minutes or until the sausage is well browned and no longer pink. Remove the skillet from the heat and drain all the grease from the sausage.

Preheat the oven to 350°. Spray a 9 x 13 casserole dish with non stick cooking spray. Spread the potatoes in the bottom of the casserole dish. Sprinkle the Italian sausage, Monterey Jack cheese, green onion and green chiles over the potatoes.

In a mixing bowl, add the eggs, whole milk, salt and black pepper. Whisk until well combined and pour over the potatoes. Do not stir. Bake for 30 minutes. Sprinkle the Parmesan cheese over the top. Bake for 15 minutes or until the potatoes are tender and the top lightly browned. Remove the casserole from the oven and serve.

Italian Sausage Chili Pasta Bake

Makes 4 servings

8 cups water
1 1/2 cups dry penne pasta
8 oz. ground Italian pork sausage
1/2 cup chopped onion
1 tsp. dried oregano
1/2 tsp. Cajun seasoning
1 cup V-8 juice
15 oz. can chili beans
14 oz. can chili style tomatoes

In a sauce pan over medium heat, add the water. When the water is boiling, add the penne pasta. Cook for 7 minutes or until the pasta is tender. Remove the pan from the heat and drain all the water from the pasta.

In a large skillet over medium heat, add the Italian sausage and onion. Stir frequently to break the sausage into crumbles as it cooks. Cook for 8 minutes or until the sausage is well browned and no longer pink. Drain any excess grease from the sausage.

Stir in the oregano and Cajun seasoning. Stir constantly and cook for 1 minute. Remove the skillet from the heat. Stir in the penne pasta, V-8 juice, chili beans with liquid and tomatoes with liquid. Stir until well combined and spoon into a 2 quart casserole dish. Preheat the oven to 350°.

Cover the dish with a lid or aluminum foil. Bake for 50 minutes or until the casserole is hot and bubbly. Remove the dish from the oven and serve.

Italian Sausage and Ravioli Casserole

Makes 6 servings

8 oz. ground Italian sausage
24 oz. jar tomato and basil spaghetti sauce
6 oz. pkg. fresh baby spinach
1/2 cup refrigerated pesto sauce
25 oz. pkg. frozen cheese ravioli
1 cup shredded Italian cheese blend

In a skillet over medium heat, add the Italian sausage. Stir frequently to break the sausage into crumbles as it cooks. Cook for 8 minutes or until the sausage is well browned and no longer pink. Remove the skillet from the heat and drain all the grease from the sausage. Add the spaghetti sauce to the skillet and stir until combined.

Preheat the oven to 375°. Chop the spinach and add to a mixing bowl. Add the pesto sauce and toss until combined. Spray a 11 x 7 casserole dish with non stick cooking spray. Spoon 1/2 cup sausage in the bottom of the casserole dish. Spread half the spinach mixture over the sausage. Place half the ravioli over the spinach. Repeat the layering process one more time. Sprinkle the remaining sausage over the top.

Bake for 30 minutes. Sprinkle the Italian cheese blend over the top. Bake for 10 minutes or until the casserole is hot and bubbly. Remove the casserole from the oven and serve.

Layered Rigatoni Casserole

Makes 8 servings

12 cups water
3 cups dry rigatoni pasta
1 lb. ground Italian sausage
28 oz. can crushed tomatoes
3 garlic cloves, minced
1 tbs. dried basil
3 cups sliced fresh mushrooms
7 oz. jar diced roasted red bell peppers, drained
1 cup shredded Parmesan cheese
2 1/2 cups shredded mozzarella cheese

In a sauce pan over medium heat, add the water. When the water is boiling, add the rigatoni pasta. Cook for 6 minutes or until the pasta is tender. Remove the pan from the heat and drain all the water from the pasta.

Spray a 9 x 13 casserole dish with non stick cooking spray. Preheat the oven to 375°. In a skillet over medium heat, add the Italian sausage. Stir frequently to break the sausage into crumbles as it cooks. Cook for 8 minutes or until the sausage is well browned and no longer pink. Remove the skillet from the heat and drain all the grease from the sausage.

In a mixing bowl, add the crushed tomatoes, garlic and basil. Stir until combined. Spread half the rigatoni pasta in the bottom of the casserole dish. Sprinkle half the Italian sausage, mushrooms, roasted red bell peppers and Parmesan cheese over the pasta. Spread half the tomato sauce over the top. Sprinkle half the mozzarella cheese over the top. Repeat the layering process using the remaining pasta, Italian sausage, mushrooms, roasted red bell peppers, Parmesan cheese, tomato sauce and mozzarella cheese.

Bake for 40 minutes or until the casserole is hot and bubbly. The mozzarella cheese should be golden brown when ready. Remove the dish from the oven and serve.

Baked Ziti Casserole

Makes 6 servings

15 oz. carton ricotta cheese
2 beaten eggs
1/2 tsp. dried basil
1/2 tsp. dried oregano
1/2 tsp. dried parsley
1/2 tsp. black pepper
1/4 tsp. garlic powder
1 1/2 cups spaghetti sauce
6 cups cooked ziti pasta
1 lb. ground Italian sausage, cooked
2 cups shredded mozzarella cheese

In a mixing bowl, add the ricotta cheese, eggs, basil, oregano, parsley, black pepper and garlic powder. Stir until well combined. Preheat the oven to 375°. Spray a 9 x 13 baking dish with non stick cooking spray.

Spread the spaghetti sauce in the bottom of the dish. Spoon the ziti pasta over the sauce. Place the Italian sausage over the pasta. Spread the ricotta mixture over the top of the dish. Sprinkle the mozzarella cheese over the top.

Place a lid or aluminum foil over the casserole. Bake for 20 minutes. Remove the lid or aluminum foil. Bake for 20 minutes or until the casserole is hot and bubbly. Remove the dish from the oven and cool for 5 minutes before serving.

Southwest Sausage Casserole

Makes a 9 x 13 casserole dish

6 flour tortillas, 10" size
4 cans diced green chiles, 4 oz. size
1 lb. ground pork sausage, cooked
2 cups shredded Pepper Jack cheese
10 eggs
1/2 cup whole milk
1/2 tsp. salt
1/2 tsp. garlic salt
1/2 tsp. onion salt
1/2 tsp. black pepper
1/2 tsp. ground cumin
2 tomatoes, sliced

Cut the tortillas into 1/2" strips. Drain the green chiles of all liquid. Spray a 9 x 13 casserole dish with non stick cooking spray. Place half the tortilla strips in the casserole dish. Spread half the green chiles over the tortillas. Spread half the sausage over the tortillas. Sprinkle 1 cup Pepper Jack cheese over the tortillas. Repeat the layering process one more time using the remaining tortillas, green chiles, sausage and Pepper Jack cheese.

In a mixing bowl, add the eggs, milk, salt, garlic salt, onion salt, black pepper and cumin. Whisk until combined and pour over the casserole. Cover the dish and refrigerate the casserole for 8 hours. Remove the casserole from the refrigerator and let the casserole sit for 30 minutes at room temperature.

Preheat the oven to 350°. Bake for 50 minutes. Place the tomato slices over the top of the casserole. Bake for 15 minutes or until a knife inserted in the center of the casserole comes out clean. Remove the dish from the oven and cool for 5 minutes before serving.

Italian Sausage Brunch Casserole

Makes 12 servings

1/2 cup softened unsalted butter
16 slices bread, crust removed
4 cups sliced mushrooms
2 cups sliced onion
Salt and black pepper to taste
1 lb. ground Italian sausage, cooked
3 cups shredded cheddar cheese
5 eggs
2 1/2 cups whole milk
1 tbs. Dijon mustard
1 tsp. ground nutmeg
1 tsp. dry mustard
2 tbs. minced fresh parsley

Spray a 9 x 13 casserole dish with non stick cooking spray. Spread 1/4 cup butter on one side of each bread slice. Place 8 bread slices, butter side down, in the casserole dish. In a large skillet over medium heat, add 1/4 cup butter, mushrooms and onion. Saute the vegetables for 10 minutes. Remove the skillet from the heat and spoon half the mushrooms and onion over the bread slices.

Sprinkle half the sausage and 1 1/2 cups cheddar cheese over the bread slices. Repeat the layering process one more time using the remaining bread slices, mushrooms and onions, sausage and cheddar cheese.

In a mixing bowl, add the eggs, milk, Dijon mustard, nutmeg and dry mustard. Season to taste with salt and black pepper. Whisk until combined and pour over the top of the casserole. Cover the dish with a lid or aluminum foil. Refrigerate the casserole for 8 hours.

Remove the casserole from the refrigerator and let the casserole sit for 30 minutes at room temperature. Preheat the oven to 350°. Leave the cover on the dish. Bake for 50 minutes. Remove the lid or aluminum foil from the dish. Sprinkle the parsley over the top of the dish. Bake for 15 minutes or until a knife inserted in the center of the casserole comes out clean. Remove the casserole from the oven and serve.

Italian Brunch Bake

Makes a 9 x 13 casserole dish

8 oz. sweet Italian sausage, casings removed
1 cup sliced green onion
3 cups sliced zucchini
1 tsp. salt
1/2 tsp. black pepper
7 oz. jar roasted red bell peppers, drained and chopped
8 cups Italian bread, cubed
2 cups shredded sharp cheddar cheese
6 eggs
1 1/2 cups whole milk

In a skillet over medium heat, add the sausage. Stir frequently to break the sausage into crumbles as it cooks. Cook for 8 minutes or until the sausage is well browned and no longer pink. Drain the excess grease from the sausage. Remove the sausage from the skillet and set aside.

Add the green onions, zucchini, salt and black pepper to the skillet. Saute the vegetables for 5 minutes. Remove the skillet from the heat and cool the zucchini for 10 minutes.

Spray a 9 x 13 casserole dish with non stick cooking spray. Place 4 cups bread cubes in the casserole dish. Spoon half the sausage over the bread. Spoon half the vegetable mixture over the bread. Sprinkle half the cheddar cheese over the bread. Repeat the layering process one more time using the remaining bread, sausage, vegetables and cheese.

In a mixing bowl, add the eggs and milk. Whisk until smooth and combined. Pour the eggs over the top of the casserole. Do not stir. Cover the dish with aluminum foil. Refrigerate for 8 hours.

Remove the casserole from the refrigerator and let the casserole sit for 15 minutes at room temperature. Preheat the oven to 350°. Leave the aluminum foil on the casserole. Bake for 1 hour. Remove the aluminum foil from the dish. Bake for 5 minutes or until the dish is hot and bubbly. Remove the casserole from the oven and serve.

Creamy Prosciutto Casserole

Makes 4 servings

4 cups cooked pasta, any shape you desire
1 cup mascarpone cheese
15 oz. can green peas, drained
1 cup finely chopped prosciutto
1 1/2 cups shredded mozzarella cheese
2 tbs. unsalted butter, cut into small pieces

Preheat the oven to 350°. Spray a 9" baking dish with non stick cooking spray. Place 2 cups pasta in the bottom of the dish. Spread 1/2 cup mascarpone cheese over the pasta. Sprinkle half the green peas, 1/2 cup prosciutto and 3/4 cup mozzarella cheese over the pasta. Repeat the layering process one more time using the remaining pasta, mascarpone cheese, green peas, prosciutto and mozzarella cheese.

Place the butter over the top of the casserole. Bake for 20 minutes or until the casserole is hot and bubbly. Remove the casserole from the oven and serve.

Meaty Breakfast Custard Casserole

Makes 4 servings

2 baking potatoes, peeled and thinly sliced
Salt and black pepper to taste
8 oz. cooked pork sausage, crumbled
8 oz. cooked bacon, crumbled
1/2 cup thinly sliced roasted red bell peppers
3 eggs
1 cup whole milk
3 tbs. chopped fresh chives
1 cup chunky salsa

Preheat the oven to 375°. Spray a 9" square baking dish with non stick cooking spray. Place half the potatoes in the baking dish. Sprinkle salt and black pepper to taste over the potatoes. Sprinkle half the sausage and bacon over the potatoes. Repeat the layering process one more time using the remaining potatoes, sausage and bacon.

Place the red bell peppers over the top of the dish. In a mixing bowl, add the eggs, whole milk and chives. Season with salt and black pepper as desired. Pour the eggs over the top of the casserole. Do not stir. Cover the dish with a lid or aluminum foil.

Bake for 45 minutes. Remove the lid or aluminum foil from the dish. Bake for 10 minutes or until the potatoes are tender and the casserole set. Remove the dish from the oven and spread the salsa over the top of the dish and serve.

Italian Sausage Egg Casserole

Makes 12 servings

8 slices bread, cubed
1 lb ground Italian sausage
2 cups shredded sharp cheddar cheese
2 cups shredded mozzarella cheese
9 eggs
3 cups whole milk
1 tsp. dried basil
1 tsp. dried oregano
1 tsp. crushed fennel seed

Spray a 9 x 13 casserole dish with non stick cooking spray. Add the bread cubes to the dish. In a skillet over medium heat, add the Italian sausage. Stir frequently to break the sausage into crumbles as it cooks. Cook for 8 minutes or until the sausage is well browned and no longer pink. Remove the skillet from the heat and drain all the grease from the sausage. Spoon the sausage over the bread in the casserole dish. Sprinkle the cheddar and mozzarella cheese over the sausage and bread cubes.

In a mixing bowl, add the eggs, milk, basil, oregano and fennel seed. Whisk until combined and pour over the top of the casserole. Make sure the bread cubes are coated in the eggs. Cover the dish with a lid or aluminum foil. Refrigerate the casserole at least 8 hours but no longer than 12 hours. Remove the casserole from the refrigerator and let the casserole sit at room temperature for 30 minutes.

Preheat the oven to 350°. Remove the lid or aluminum foil from the casserole. Bake for 55 minutes or until a knife inserted in the center of the casserole comes out clean. Remove the casserole from the oven and cool for 5 minutes before serving.

Cheesy Sausage Grits Casserole

Makes 6 servings

1 lb. ground pork sausage
4 1/2 cups water
1 1/2 cups quick cooking grits
2 1/2 cups shredded cheddar cheese
3 tbs. vegetable oil
1 1/2 cups whole milk
3 beaten eggs

In a skillet over medium heat, add the sausage. Stir frequently to break the sausage into crumbles as it cooks. Cook for 8 minutes or until the sausage is well browned and no longer pink. Remove the skillet from the heat and drain all the excess grease from the sausage.

In a sauce pan over medium heat, add the water. When the water is boiling, stir in the grits. Stir constantly and cook for 5 minutes. The grits should be thick when ready. Remove the pan from the heat.

Add the cheddar cheese, vegetable oil, whole milk and eggs to the grits. Stir until well combined. Preheat the oven to 350°. Spray a 9 x 13 baking dish with non stick cooking spray. Sprinkle the sausage in the bottom of the dish. Spread the grits over the sausage. Bake for 1 hour or until the grits are set. Remove the dish from the oven and cool for 5 minutes before serving.

Smoked Sausage & Ham Noodle Casserole

Makes 4 servings

1 lb. smoked sausage, cut into 1/2" slices
4 oz. cooked ham, cubed
2 cups whole milk
2 tbs. all purpose flour
4 cups cooked penne pasta
2 1/2 cups shredded mozzarella cheese
1/3 cup grated Parmesan cheese
2 cups spaghetti sauce
1/3 cup dry breadcrumbs

In a skillet over medium heat, add the smoked sausage and ham. Stir frequently and cook until the sausage and ham are well browned. Add the milk and all purpose flour to the skillet. Stir constantly and cook until the milk comes to a boil. Remove the skillet from the heat.

Stir in the pasta, mozzarella cheese, Parmesan cheese and spaghetti sauce. Preheat the oven to 350°. Spoon the casserole into a 9 x 13 casserole dish. Cover the dish with a lid or aluminum foil. Bake for 20 minutes. Remove the lid or aluminum foil. Sprinkle the breadcrumbs over the top of the casserole. Bake for 10 minutes or until the breadcrumbs are toasted and the casserole hot and bubbly. Remove the dish from the oven and serve.

Smoked Sausage Mashed Potato Bake

Makes 6 servings

5 potatoes, peeled and quartered
1/2 cup sour cream
1/4 cup chicken broth
1 lb. cooked smoked sausage, sliced
3 cups sliced fresh mushrooms
1 cup chopped onion
1 garlic clove, minced
1/4 cup shredded cheddar cheese
1 tsp. dried parsley
1 tsp. dried oregano

In a sauce pan over medium heat, add the potatoes. Cover the potatoes with water and bring the potatoes to a boil. When the potatoes are boiling, reduce the heat to low. Simmer the potatoes for 20 minutes or until the potatoes are tender. Remove the pan from the heat. Drain all the water from the potatoes. Add the potatoes to a mixing bowl. Add the sour cream and chicken broth. Using a mixer on low speed, beat until the potatoes are smooth and combined.

In a skillet over medium heat, add the smoked sausage, mushrooms, onion and garlic. Stir frequently and cook until the smoked sausage is well browned and the vegetables tender. Remove the skillet from the heat. Drain all the excess grease from the skillet.

Preheat the oven to 350°. Spray an 8" square pan with non stick cooking spray. Spread half the mashed potatoes in the pan. Spoon the smoked sausage and vegetables over the potatoes. Spread the remaining potatoes over the smoked sausage. Sprinkle the cheddar cheese, parsley and oregano over the potatoes. Bake for 15 minutes. Remove the dish from the oven and serve.

Smoked Sausage & Beans Cornbread Casserole

Makes 6 servings

2 cans pork and beans, 15 oz. size
12 oz. cooked smoked sausage, thinly sliced
2 tbs. light brown sugar
2 tbs. Worcestershire sauce
2 tbs. yellow prepared mustard
8 oz. pkg. cornbread muffin mix
1 cup shredded cheddar cheese

Preheat the oven to 350°. Spray a 9" square baking pan with non stick cooking spray. Add the pork and beans with liquid, smoked sausage, brown sugar, Worcestershire sauce and mustard to the baking pan. Stir until combined.

Prepare the cornbread muffin batter according to package directions. Stir the cheddar cheese into the batter. Drop the batter by tablespoonfuls over the beans. Bake for 40 minutes or until the cornbread is done and golden brown. Remove the dish from the oven and serve.

You can substitute all beef hot dogs, 2 cups cooked ground beef, 2 1/2 cups diced cooked pork or cooked pork sausage links for the smoked sausage if desired.

Hominy Sausage Bake

Makes 8 servings

1 lb. smoked sausage, cut into 1/4 slices
1 tsp. olive oil
2 cups diced cooked ham
2 pkgs. dry red beans and rice mix, 8 oz. size
6 cups water
2 tbs. unsalted butter
1/4 tsp. cayenne pepper
29 oz. can yellow hominy, rinsed and drained
12 oz. jar pickled jalapeno peppers, drained and chopped
15 oz. can whole kernel corn, drained
1 cup shredded cheddar cheese
1 cup crushed corn chips

In a dutch oven over medium heat, add the smoked sausage and olive oil. Saute the smoked sausage for 5 minutes. Add the ham, red beans and rice mix, water, butter and cayenne pepper to the pan. Stir until well combined and bring the rice to a boil. When the rice is boiling, reduce the heat to low. Place a lid on the pan and simmer the rice for 20 minutes. The rice should be tender when ready. Remove the pan from the oven.

Preheat the oven to 350°. Spoon the smoked sausage mixture into a 9 x 13 casserole dish. Spread the hominy, jalapeno peppers and corn over the top of the dish. Bake for 40 minutes or until the dish is hot and bubbly. Sprinkle the corn chips and cheddar cheese over the top of the casserole. Bake for 10 minutes and remove the dish from the oven.

Smoked Sausage and Grits Casserole

Makes 12 servings

1 1/2 lbs. chopped smoked sausage
4 1/2 cups water
1/2 tsp. salt
1 1/2 cups dry quick cooking grits
4 cups shredded sharp cheddar cheese
1 cup whole milk
1 1/2 tsp. chopped fresh thyme
1/4 tsp. garlic powder
1/4 tsp. black pepper
4 beaten eggs

In a large skillet over medium heat, add the smoked sausage. Cook for 10 minutes or until the sausage is well browned and releases most of the fat from the sausage. Remove the skillet from the heat.

In a sauce pan over medium heat, add the water and salt. Bring the water to a boil and stir in the grits. Bring the grits to a boil and place a lid on the pan. Simmer the grits for 5 minutes or until they are thickened and tender. Stir occasionally while the grits are cooking. Remove the pan from the heat and stir in the cheddar cheese. Stir until the cheese is completely melted.

Preheat the oven to 350°. Spray a 9 x 13 casserole dish with non stick cooking spray. Add the milk, thyme, garlic powder, black pepper, eggs and smoked sausage to the grits. Stir until well combined and spoon into the casserole dish.

Bake for 50 minutes or until the casserole is golden brown. Remove the dish from the oven and cool for 5 minutes before serving.

Lil Smokies Macaroni and Cheese Casserole

Makes 6 servings

7 oz. box macaroni and cheese, prepared
1 lb. Lil Smokies smoked sausage
10.75 oz. can cream of mushroom soup
1/3 cup whole milk
1 tbs. minced fresh parsley
1 cup shredded cheddar cheese

Preheat the oven to 350°. Spray a 2 quart casserole dish with non stick cooking spray. Add the prepared macaroni and cheese, Lil Smokies, cream of mushroom soup, milk and parsley to a mixing bowl. Stir until well combined. Spoon the casserole into the prepared dish. Sprinkle the cheddar cheese over the top.

Bake for 20 minutes or until the casserole is hot and bubbly. Remove the dish from the oven and serve.

4 TUNA & SEAFOOD

Canned tuna and salmon are perfect for casseroles. They take the prep time out of meals. Seafood cooks quickly in a casserole making for a speedy meal.

Tuna Spaghetti Casserole

Makes 4 servings

3 quarts water
3 tsp. salt
1 tbs. vegetable oil
2 cups dry elbow macaroni
1/2 cup chopped celery
1/4 cup chopped onion
2 tbs. unsalted butter
10.75 oz. can cream of celery soup
1 1/4 cups whole milk
8 oz. flaked tuna, drained
1 tbs. chopped red bell pepper
1/2 cup dry breadcrumbs
2 tbs. melted unsalted butter

In a large sauce pan over medium heat, add the water, salt and vegetable oil. When the water is boiling, add the elbow macaroni. Cook for 6 minutes or until the macaroni is tender. Remove the pan from the heat and drain all the water from the macaroni.

In a skillet over medium heat, add the celery, onion and 2 tablespoon butter. Saute the vegetables for 5 minutes. Add the cream of celery soup, milk, tuna and red bell pepper. Stir until combined and bring the filling to a boil. Remove the skillet from the heat.

Preheat the oven to 350°. Add the elbow macaroni to the skillet. Stir until all the ingredients are combined. Spoon the casserole into a 2 quart casserole dish. In a small bowl, add the breadcrumbs and 2 tablespoons melted butter. Toss until combined and sprinkle over the casserole. Bake for 25 minutes. Remove the casserole from the oven and serve.

Tuna Vegetable Casserole

Makes 6 servings

16 oz. pkg. frozen mixed vegetables
15 oz. canned tuna, drained
1 cup dry instant rice
10.75 oz. can cream of celery soup
1 cup whole milk
1 cup Goldfish crackers

Preheat the oven to 350°. Add the mixed vegetables, tuna, rice, cream of celery soup and milk to a mixing bowl. Stir until well combined. Spray a 3 quart casserole dish with non stick cooking spray. Spoon the casserole into the dish.

Bake for 30 minutes or until the vegetables are tender. Remove the casserole from the oven and sprinkle the Goldfish crackers over the top. Cool the casserole for 5 minutes before serving.

Mushroom Tuna Bake

Makes 6 servings

10.75 oz. can cream of celery soup
1 cup whole milk
1 cup cooked sliced mushrooms
1/2 cup freshly grated Parmesan cheese
1 tsp. dried Italian seasoning
1/2 tsp. season salt
1/4 tsp. garlic powder
12 oz. solid white tuna, drained and flaked
3 cups cooked egg noodles
1 cup croutons, coarsely crushed

Preheat the oven to 350°. Spray a 11 x 7 casserole dish with non stick cooking spray. In a mixing bowl, add the cream of celery soup, milk, mushrooms, 1/4 cup Parmesan cheese, Italian seasoning, season salt and garlic powder. Stir until well combined.

Add the tuna and egg noodles to the bowl. Toss until combined. Spoon the casserole into the prepared dish. Bake for 20 minutes. Sprinkle 1/4 cup Parmesan cheese and croutons over the casserole. Bake for 15 minutes or until the casserole is hot and bubbly. Remove the casserole from the oven and cool for 5 minutes before serving.

Salmon Stroganoff

Makes 4 servings

4 cups cooked egg noodles
14 oz. can salmon, drained and bones removed
2 cups sliced cooked mushrooms
1/4 cup finely chopped red bell pepper
1 1/2 cups cottage cheese
1 1/2 cups sour cream
1/2 cup mayonnaise
3 tbs. grated onion
1 garlic clove, minced
1 1/2 tsp. Worcestershire sauce
1 tsp. salt
1 cup shredded cheddar cheese
1/3 cup dry breadcrumbs
2 tbs. melted unsalted butter

Spray a 2 quart casserole dish with non stick cooking spray. Preheat the oven to 350°. Add the egg noodles, salmon, mushrooms, red bell pepper, cottage cheese, sour cream, mayonnaise, onion, garlic, Worcestershire sauce, salt and cheddar cheese to the casserole dish. Stir until well combined.

In a small bowl, add the breadcrumbs and butter. Toss until the breadcrumbs are coated in the butter. Sprinkle the breadcrumbs over the top of the casserole. Bake for 30 minutes or until the casserole is hot and bubbly. Remove the dish from the oven and serve.

Greek Shrimp and Pasta Bake

Makes 6 servings

2 quarts water
2 1/2 cups dry penne pasta
3/4 lb. fresh shrimp, peeled and deveined
3 cups fresh spinach leaves, stems removed
1 cup cherry tomatoes, halved
1 tsp. salt
1 tsp. dried oregano
2 tbs. olive oil
1 cup crumbled feta cheese
1/4 cup sliced black olives

In a dutch oven over medium heat, add the water. When the water is boiling, add the penne pasta. Cook for 3 minutes. Add the shrimp to the pan. Cook for 4 minutes or until the pasta is tender and shrimp turn pink. Remove the pan from the heat and drain all the water from the pasta.

Preheat the oven to 350°. Spray a 9 x 13 baking pan with non stick cooking spray. Add the spinach, tomatoes, salt, oregano, olive oil, feta cheese and black olives to the pasta and shrimp. Stir until all the ingredients are combined.

Spoon the casserole in the baking pan. Bake for 15 minutes or until the casserole is thoroughly heated. Remove the pan from the oven and serve.

Mediterranean Snapper Casserole

Makes 6 servings

2 onions, sliced
2 red bell peppers, thinly sliced
2 tbs. olive oil
2 large tomatoes, cut into thin wedges
3 garlic cloves, minced
2 lbs. red snapper fillets
Salt and black pepper to taste
8 oz. crumbled feta cheese
1 tbs. chopped fresh parsley

Preheat the oven to 375°. In a large skillet over medium heat, add the onion, red bell peppers and olive oil. Saute the vegetables for 5 minutes. Add the tomatoes and garlic to the skillet. Stir until combined and remove the skillet from the heat.

Place the red snapper fillets in a 9 x 13 baking dish. Season the fish to taste with salt and black pepper. Spoon the vegetables from the skillet over the fillets. Sprinkle the feta cheese over the top of the casserole. Bake for 25 minutes or until the fish flakes easily with a fork. Remove the dish from the oven and sprinkle the parsley over the top before serving.

5 BEANS, VEGETABLES, SIDES & MEATLESS CASSEROLES

My family eats a meatless meal twice a week. We strive to add more vegetables to our diet while still satisfying our homestyle southern appetite. Vegetable casseroles are great for a side dish or a main dish meal. I frequently prepare several vegetable casseroles for dinner. I round out the meal with fresh fruit and rolls. With the holidays rapidly approaching, easy side dishes are just the ticket.

Baked Macaroni and Cheese

Makes a 9 x 13 casserole dish

2 cups dry elbow macaroni
1/2 cup melted unsalted butter
3 cups shredded cheddar cheese
1 cup shredded mozzarella cheese
5 cups whole milk
Salt and black pepper taste

Preheat the oven to 350°. Spray a 9 x 13 casserole dish with non stick cooking spray. Spread the macaroni in the bottom of the dish. Drizzle the butter over the macaroni. Sprinkle the cheddar and mozzarella cheese over the macaroni. Pour the milk over the cheeses and macaroni. Season with salt and black pepper to taste. You do not have to stir the dish unless desired.

Bake for 1 hour or until the macaroni is tender and most of the milk absorbed. The cheeses make a crusty top. You can cover the dish with a lid or aluminum foil during the last 20 minutes of cooking time if you do not want a crusty top. Remove the dish from the oven and serve.

Caramelized Onion Macaroni & Cheese Casserole

Makes 8 servings

4 tbs. melted unsalted butter
4 cups thinly sliced onion
1 tsp. granulated sugar
4 cups cooked elbow macaroni
4 cups shredded white cheddar cheese
1 cup shredded Parmesan cheese
32 saltine crackers, finely crushed
6 eggs
4 cups whole milk
1 tsp. salt
1/2 tsp. black pepper

In a large skillet over medium heat, add 2 tablespoons butter, onions and granulated sugar. Saute the onions for 20 minutes or until the onions are caramelized. Remove the skillet from the heat.

Spray a 9 x 13 casserole dish with non stick cooking spray. Place half the elbow macaroni in the bottom of the casserole dish. Sprinkle half the white cheddar cheese, Parmesan cheese and saltine crackers over the macaroni. Sprinkle the remaining macaroni over the top of the casserole. Sprinkle the remaining white cheddar and Parmesan cheese over the macaroni.

In a mixing bowl, add the eggs, milk, salt and black pepper. Whisk until well combined and pour over the top of the casserole. Sprinkle the remaining cracker crumbs over the top of the casserole. Drizzle 2 tablespoons butter over the cracker crumbs.

Bake for 1 hour or until the casserole is golden brown. Remove the dish from the oven and cool for 10 minutes before serving.

Monterey Spaghetti Casserole

Makes 4 servings

1 cup sour cream
1 beaten egg
2 cups cooked spaghetti noodles
2 cups shredded Monterey Jack cheese
1/4 cup grated Parmesan cheese
10 oz. pkg. frozen spinach, thawed and drained
1 1/3 cups french fried onions

Preheat the oven to 350°. Add the sour cream and egg to an 8" square baking dish. Whisk until well combined. Add the noodles, Monterey Jack cheese, Parmesan cheese, spinach and 2/3 cup french fried onions. Stir until combined.

Cover the dish with a lid or aluminum foil. Bake for 30 minutes or until the dish is bubbly. Remove the lid or aluminum foil. Sprinkle 2/3 cup french fried onions over the top of the casserole. Bake for 5 minutes or until the french fried onions are toasted. Remove the casserole from the oven and serve.

Cornbread Dumpling Vegetable Cobbler

Makes a 9 x 13 casserole dish

2 lbs. butternut squash, peeled and cubed
1 lb. red potatoes, cut into 1/2" wedges
3 parsnips, peeled and cut into 1/2" pieces
1 purple onion, peeled and cut into 1/2" wedges
3 tbs. olive oil
1 tsp. salt
1 tsp. dried tarragon
14 oz. can vegetable broth
2 cups fresh broccoli florets
1/2 tsp. grated lemon zest
4 tsp. cornstarch
1 1/2 cups whole milk
1 3/4 cups Bisquick
1/2 cup plain yellow cornmeal
1/8 tsp. cayenne pepper

Add the butternut squash, red potatoes, parsnips and purple onion to a 9 x 13 casserole dish. In a small bowl, stir together the olive oil, salt and tarragon. Drizzle over the vegetables. Toss until the vegetables are coated in the oil and seasonings.

Preheat the oven to 375°. Bake for 1 hour or until the vegetables are tender. In a sauce pan over medium heat, add the vegetable broth, broccoli and lemon zest. Bring the broccoli to a boil and cook for 2 minutes. In a small bowl, add the cornstarch and 1/2 cup milk. Whisk until combined and add to the broccoli. Stir constantly and cook until the sauce thickens and bubbles. Remove the pan from the heat. Spoon the broccoli and sauce over the roasted vegetables. Stir until combined.

In a mixing bowl, add 1 cup whole milk, Bisquick, cornmeal and cayenne pepper. Stir until combined and drop by tablespoonfuls over the vegetables. Bake for 20 minutes or until the dumplings are golden brown. Remove the dish from the oven and serve.

Vegetable Bread Pudding Casserole

Makes a 9 x 13 casserole dish

1 lb. loaf Italian bread, cubed
14 oz. can diced tomatoes
10 oz. pkg. frozen chopped spinach, thawed and drained
1 cup chopped fresh mushrooms
1 cup shredded mozzarella cheese
1/2 cup chopped green bell pepper
1/2 cup chopped zucchini
2 green onions, chopped
1 tsp. dried basil
1/2 tsp. dried oregano
1 cup whole milk
4 eggs
1 tsp. salt
1/4 tsp. black pepper

Spray a 9 x 13 casserole dish with non stick cooking spray. In a mixing bowl, add the Italian bread cubes, tomatoes with juice, spinach, mushrooms, mozzarella cheese, green bell pepper, zucchini, green onions, basil and oregano. Toss until well combined and spoon into the casserole dish.

In a mixing bowl, add the milk, eggs, salt and black pepper. Whisk until combined and pour over the top of the casserole. Cover the dish with a lid or aluminum foil. Refrigerate for 2 hours but no longer than 10 hours.

Remove the dish from the refrigerator and let the casserole sit for 30 minutes at room temperature. Preheat the oven to 400°. Do not remove the lid or aluminum foil. Bake for 15 minutes. Remove the lid or aluminum foil. Bake for 15 minutes or until a knife inserted in the center of the dish comes out clean. Remove the dish from the oven and serve.

Vegetable Medley Casserole

Makes a 9 x 13 casserole dish

1 head cauliflower, cut into florets
1 head broccoli, cut into florets
6 carrots, sliced
8 cups sliced mushrooms
8 green onions, sliced
1/4 cup unsalted butter, cubed
10.75 oz. can cream of chicken soup
1/2 cup whole milk
1/2 cup Velveeta cheese sauce

In a dutch oven over medium heat, add the cauliflower, broccoli and carrots. Cover the vegetables with water and bring the vegetables to a boil. When the vegetables are boiling, cook for 6 minutes. The vegetables should be crisp tender when ready. Remove the pan from the heat and drain all the water from the pan.

In a skillet over medium heat, add the mushrooms, green onions and butter. Stir constantly and cook until the mushrooms are tender. Remove the skillet from the heat. Add the mushrooms to the vegetable mixture. Add the cream of chicken soup, milk and cheese sauce to the vegetables. Stir until combined.

Spoon the vegetables and sauce into a 9 x 13 casserole dish. Preheat the oven to 350°. Bake for 30 minutes or until the casserole is hot and bubbly. Remove the casserole from the oven and serve.

Zucchini Ricotta Casserole

Makes 8 servings

15 oz. carton ricotta cheese
2 eggs
1/2 cup dry breadcrumbs
5 tbs. grated Parmesan cheese
1 tbs. minced fresh parsley
1/4 tsp. dried oregano
1/4 tsp. dried basil
1/8 tsp. black pepper
26 oz. jar spaghetti sauce
6 cups zucchini, cut into 1/4" slices
1 1/2 cups shredded mozzarella cheese

Spray a 9 x 13 casserole dish with non stick cooking spray. Preheat the oven to 350°. In a mixing bowl, add the ricotta cheese, eggs, 3 tablespoons breadcrumbs, 3 tablespoons Parmesan cheese, parsley, oregano, basil and black pepper. Whisk until well combined.

Spread 1/3 of the spaghetti sauce in the bottom of the casserole dish. Sprinkle 2 tablespoons breadcrumbs over the sauce. Place 3 cups zucchini slices over the sauce. Spread half the ricotta cheese mixture over the zucchini. Sprinkle 3/4 cup mozzarella cheese over the ricotta. Spread half of the remaining sauce over the top of the cheeses. Place the remaining zucchini slices over the sauce. Spread the remaining ricotta cheese mixture and mozzarella cheese over the zucchini. Spread the remaining spaghetti sauce over the top.

Sprinkle 2 tablespoons Parmesan cheese and the remaining breadcrumbs over the top of the dish. Place a lid or aluminum foil over the dish. Preheat the oven to 350°. Bake for 45 minutes. Remove the lid or aluminum foil. Bake for 20 minutes or until the zucchini is tender and the casserole bubbly. Remove the dish from the oven and cool for 10 minutes before serving.

Butternut Squash Casserole

Makes 6 servings

2 medium butternut squash, peeled and cubed
1/2 cup granulated sugar
2 eggs
1/4 cup whole milk
2 tbs. unsalted butter
1 tsp. vanilla extract
1/4 tsp. ground cinnamon
1/4 tsp. ground nutmeg

In a large sauce pan over medium heat, add the butternut squash. Cover the squash with water. Bring the squash to a boil and cook for 15 minutes or until the squash is tender. Remove the pan from the heat and drain all the water from the pan.

Mash the squash until smooth. Add the granulated sugar, eggs, milk, butter, vanilla extract, cinnamon and nutmeg to the squash. Stir until all the ingredients are well combined.

Preheat the oven to 350°. Spoon the squash into a 1 1/2 quart casserole dish. Bake for 35 minutes or until the casserole is set and bubbly. Remove the dish from the oven and serve.

Cheesy Vegetable Pasta Casserole

Makes 6 servings

16 oz. pkg. frozen peas and carrots
1 cup shredded mozzarella cheese
1/2 cup cubed provolone cheese
1 1/2 cups french fried onions
3 cups cooked fettuccine noodles
10.75 oz. can cream of mushroom soup
3/4 cup whole milk
1/2 tsp. garlic salt
1/3 cup grated Parmesan cheese

Preheat the oven to 350°. Spray a 9 x 13 casserole dish with non stick cooking spray. Add the peas and carrots, mozzarella cheese, provolone cheese, 2/3 cup fried onions and fettuccine noodles to the dish. Stir until combined.

In a mixing bowl, add the cream of mushroom soup, milk, garlic salt and Parmesan cheese. Stir until combined and pour over the top of the casserole. Do not stir.

Cover the dish with a lid or aluminum foil. Bake for 30 minutes or until the peas and carrots are tender. Remove the lid or aluminum foil. Sprinkle the remaining fried onions over the top of the dish. Bake for 10 minutes. Remove the dish from the oven and serve.

Biscuit Mushroom Bake

Makes 4 servings

8 cups sliced fresh mushrooms
2 tbs. unsalted butter
3 tbs. all purpose flour
1 cup chicken broth
1/2 cup whole milk
1 tbs. lemon juice
1 tsp. onion powder
1 tsp. garlic powder
1/4 tsp. salt
1/4 tsp. black pepper
1/4 tsp. paprika
8 ct. can refrigerated biscuits

In a 10" oven proof skillet over medium heat, add the mushrooms and butter. Saute the mushrooms for 10 minutes or until they are tender. Sprinkle the all purpose flour over the mushrooms. Stir constantly and cook for 1 minute. Add the chicken broth and milk to the skillet. Stir constantly and cook until the sauce thickens and bubbles. Remove the skillet from the heat. Stir in the lemon juice, onion powder, garlic powder, salt, black pepper and paprika.

Preheat the oven to 375°. Remove the biscuits from the can and place over the mushrooms. Bake for 20 minutes or until the biscuits are golden brown. Remove the dish from the oven and serve hot.

Tex Mex Black Bean Ravioli Casserole

Makes 6 servings

2 cups salsa
10.75 oz. can crushed tomatoes
1/2 tsp. ground cumin
28 oz. bag frozen cheese ravioli
5 cups cooked black beans, rinsed and drained
1/2 cup chopped fresh cilantro
8 green onions, thinly sliced
2 cups shredded sharp cheddar cheese
1 cup shredded Monterey Jack cheese

Spray a 11 x 7 baking dish with non stick cooking spray. In a mixing bowl, add the salsa, crushed tomatoes and cumin. Stir until combined. Pour 1/2 cup sauce into the baking dish. Place the ravioli over the sauce. Spoon the black beans, cilantro and green onions over the ravioli. Spread the remaining sauce over the top of the dish.

Sprinkle the cheddar and Monterey Jack cheese over the top of the casserole. Cover the dish with a lid or aluminum foil. Preheat the oven to 350°. Bake for 45 minutes or until the dish is hot, bubbly and the ravioli tender. Remove the aluminum foil and bake for 5 minutes. Remove the dish from the oven and serve.

Rice and Black Bean Casserole

Makes 4 servings

15 oz. can black beans, rinsed and drained
10 oz. can diced tomatoes with green chiles
1 cup tomato sauce
1 cup picante sauce
2 cups cooked rice
1 cup sour cream
2 cup shredded cheddar cheese
2 cups crushed tortilla chips

Preheat the oven to 350°. Spray a 9 x 13 casserole dish with non stick cooking spray. Add the black beans, tomatoes with juice, tomato sauce, picante sauce, rice, sour cream and cheddar cheese to the casserole dish. Stir until combined. Bake for 20 minutes or until the casserole is hot and bubbly.

Sprinkle the tortilla chips over the top of the casserole. Bake for 5 minutes. Remove the dish from the oven and serve.

Mexican Rice and Cheese Casserole

Makes a 9 x 13 casserole dish

16 oz. pkg. dry Mexican rice mix, prepared
2 cups shredded Monterey Jack cheese
1 cup thinly sliced green onions
1 tsp. salt
1/4 tsp. cayenne pepper
1/4 tsp. smoked paprika

Preheat the oven to 350°. Spray a 9 x 13 casserole dish with non stick cooking spray. Add the prepared rice mix, 1 1/2 cups Monterey Jack cheese, green onions, salt and cayenne pepper to the casserole dish. Stir until combined.

Sprinkle the paprika over the top of the casserole. Sprinkle 1/2 cup Monterey Jack cheese over the top of the rice. Bake for 30 minutes. The rice should be heated and the cheese melted when ready. Remove the dish from the oven and serve.

Easy Onion Potato Casserole

Makes 12 servings

32 oz. pkg. frozen hashbrowns, thawed
2 cups sour cream
2 cups shredded cheddar cheese
10.75 oz. can cream of chicken soup
1 cup chopped green onions
3 oz. can fried onions

Preheat the oven to 375°. Spray a 9 x 13 casserole dish with non stick cooking spray. In a large bowl, add the hashbrowns, sour cream, cheddar cheese, cream of chicken soup and green onions. Stir until combined and spread in the casserole dish.

Bake for 20 minutes. Sprinkle the fried onions over the top. Bake for 15 minutes or until the casserole is hot, bubbly and the hashbrowns tender. Remove the casserole from the oven and serve.

Potato and Gruyere Casserole

Makes 12 servings

8 cups peeled potatoes, thinly sliced
1 1/4 tsp. salt
1/4 cup plus 2 tbs. unsalted butter
1 cup chopped onion
1/2 tsp. black pepper
1/3 cup all purpose flour
2 1/2 cups whole milk
1 cup chicken broth
2 cups shredded Gruyere cheese

In a large sauce pan over medium heat, add the potatoes and 1 teaspoon salt. Cover the potatoes with water and bring the potatoes to a boil. Cook for 8 minutes or until the potatoes are tender. Remove the pan from the heat and drain all the water from the potatoes.

In a skillet over medium heat, add 2 tablespoons butter and the onion. Saute the onion for 15 minutes or until the onion is golden brown. Remove the onion from the skillet and set aside.

Add 1/4 cup butter to the skillet. When the butter melts, add the all purpose flour. Stir constantly and cook for 1 minute. Add the milk, chicken broth and 1/4 teaspoon salt to the pan. Stir constantly and cook until the sauce thickens and bubbles. Remove the pan from the heat.

Preheat the oven to 350°. Spray a 9 x 13 casserole dish with non stick cooking spray. Place half the potatoes in the bottom of the casserole dish. Sprinkle half the onion and Gruyere cheese over the potatoes. Spread half the cream sauce over the top of the potatoes. Repeat the layering process one more time.

Bake for 1 hour or until the casserole is bubbly and golden brown. Remove the dish from the oven and serve.

Mashed Potato Casserole

Makes 4 servings

1 1/2 cups water
3 tbs. unsalted butter
1/2 cup whole milk
1 1/2 cups dry mashed potato flakes
1/2 cup sour cream
1/2 tsp. onion salt
1 egg
1/2 cup shredded American cheese

Preheat the oven to 350°. Butter a 1 1/2 quart casserole dish with 1 tablespoon butter. In a sauce pan over medium heat, add the water and 2 tablespoons butter. Bring the water to a boil and remove the pan from the heat.

Stir in the milk and mashed potato flakes. Stir until the potatoes are smooth. Add the sour cream, onion salt and egg to the potatoes. Stir until all the ingredients are well combined. Spoon the potatoes into the casserole dish. Sprinkle the American cheese over the top.

Bake for 15 minutes. Remove the dish from the oven and serve.

Mexican Potato Casserole

Makes 12 servings

32 oz. pkg. frozen hashbrowns, thawed
2 cups sour cream
2 cups shredded Mexican seasoned cheese
10.75 oz. can cream of chicken soup
4 oz. can diced green chiles, drained
2 cups crushed tortilla chips
1 cup salsa

Preheat the oven to 375°. Spray a 9 x 13 casserole dish with non stick cooking spray. In a large bowl, add the hashbrowns, sour cream, Mexican cheese, cream of chicken soup and green chiles. Stir until combined and spread in the casserole dish.

Bake for 20 minutes. Sprinkle the tortilla chips over the top. Bake for 15 minutes or until the casserole is hot, bubbly and the hashbrowns tender. Remove the casserole from the oven and drizzle the salsa over the top of the dish before serving.

Swiss Potato Casserole

Makes 8 servings

8 peeled potatoes, cubed
1/3 cup melted unsalted butter
1 tbs. minced fresh parsley
1 1/2 tsp. salt
1/4 tsp. black pepper
1 1/2 cups shredded Swiss cheese
1 cup cooked cubed ham
1/2 cup grated onion
1 tsp. garlic powder
3 eggs
1/2 cup whole milk
Paprika to taste

In a sauce pan over medium heat, add the potatoes. Cover the potatoes with water and bring the potatoes to a boil. Cook for 15 minutes or until the potatoes are tender. Remove the pan from the heat and drain all the water from the potatoes. Add the butter, parsley, salt and black pepper to the potatoes. Using a potato masher, mash until the potatoes are smooth and creamy.

Spray an 8" square pan with non stick cooking spray. Spread half the mashed potatoes in the bottom of the pan. In a small bowl, add the Swiss cheese, ham, onion and garlic powder. Stir until combined and spread over the potatoes.

In a small bowl, whisk together the eggs and milk. Pour the mixture over the top of the dish. Spread the remaining potatoes over the top of the casserole. Sprinkle paprika to taste over the top. Preheat the oven to 400°. Bake for 45 minutes. Remove the dish from the oven and cool for 5 minutes before serving.

Garlic Potato Casserole

Makes 12 servings

10 potatoes, peeled and cubed
1 tbs. vegetable oil
1/2 cup diced red bell pepper
4 garlic cloves, minced
1 cup diced green bell pepper
1 tbs. finely chopped onion
1 slice bread, finely chopped
1/2 cup melted unsalted butter
1 tsp. salt
1/2 tsp. black pepper
1/2 cup whole milk
2 cups shredded cheddar cheese
3/4 cup crushed garlic croutons

In a large sauce pan over medium heat, add the potatoes. Cook for 12 minutes or until the potatoes are tender. Remove the pan from the heat and drain all the water from the potatoes. Spray a 9 x 13 casserole dish with non stick cooking spray. Spread the potatoes in the casserole dish.

In a skillet over medium heat, add the vegetable oil. When the oil is hot, add the red bell pepper, garlic, green bell pepper and onion. Saute the vegetables for 5 minutes or until they are tender. Remove the skillet from the heat.

Add the bread, butter, salt, black pepper, milk and cheddar cheese to the skillet. Stir until well combined and pour over the potatoes. Do not stir. Sprinkle the garlic croutons over the top of the dish.

Preheat the oven to 325°. Bake for 1 hour. Remove the dish from the oven and serve.

Sweet Potato Carrot Casserole

Makes 8 servings

6 large sweet potatoes
3 cups sliced carrots
1/4 cup unsalted butter
1 cup sour cream
3 tbs. granulated sugar
1 tsp. lemon zest
1/2 tsp. salt
1/2 tsp. ground nutmeg
1/2 tsp. black pepper
1 1/2 cups miniature marshmallows
1 cup chopped pecans
1/2 tsp. ground cinnamon

Preheat the oven to 350°. Place the sweet potatoes on a baking pan. Bake for 1 hour or until the sweet potatoes are fork tender. Remove the sweet potatoes from the oven and cool for 30 minutes.

In a sauce pan over medium heat, add the carrots. Cover the carrots with water. Cook for 20 minutes or until the carrots are tender. Remove the carrots from the heat and drain all the water from the carrots.

Add the carrots and butter to a food processor. Process until smooth. Spoon the carrots into a large bowl. Remove the sweet potatoes from the skins and add to the mixing bowl. Mash the sweet potatoes and carrots until smooth.

Stir in the sour cream, 2 tablespoons granulated sugar, lemon zest, salt, nutmeg and black pepper. Stir until combined. Preheat the oven to 350°. Spoon the sweet potatoes into a 9 x 13 baking dish. Sprinkle the marshmallows over the top. Bake for 30 minutes.

In a small bowl, add the pecans, 1 tablespoon granulated sugar and cinnamon. Toss until combined and sprinkle over the marshmallows. Bake for 10 minutes. Remove the dish from the oven and serve.

Curried Cauliflower and Green Pea Casserole

Makes 6 servings

2 pkgs. frozen cauliflower florets, 10 oz. size
1 pkg. frozen green peas, 10 oz. size
1 tsp. salt
2 tbs. unsalted butter
2 tbs. all purpose flour
1 1/2 cups sour cream
1 tsp. onion salt
1 tsp. curry powder
1/2 cup slivered almonds

In a large sauce pan, add the cauliflower, green peas and salt. Cover the vegetables with water and place the pan over medium heat. Bring the vegetables to a boil and cook about 5 minutes or until the vegetables are crisp tender. Remove the pan from the heat and drain all the water from the vegetables.

Preheat the oven to 325°. Spray a 1 1/2 quart casserole dish with non stick cooking spray. In a small sauce pan over medium heat, add 1 tablespoon butter. When the butter melts, add the all purpose flour. Stir constantly and cook for 1 minute. Reduce the heat to low and stir in the sour cream. Cook only until the sauce is heated. Do not let the sauce boil once you add the sour cream. Remove the pan from the heat and stir in the onion salt.

Add the vegetables and sauce to the casserole dish. Toss until the vegetables are coated in the sauce. In a small skillet over medium heat, add 1 tablespoon butter. When the butter melts, add the curry powder and almonds. Stir constantly and cook about 5 minutes or until the almonds are toasted. Remove the skillet from the heat and spoon the almonds over the vegetables.

Bake the casserole for 25 minutes. Remove the dish from the oven and serve.

Poblano Cheese Casserole

Makes 6 servings

6 large poblano chile peppers
16 oz. container ricotta cheese
1 1/2 cups shredded Monterey Jack cheese
1 1/2 cups shredded mozzarella cheese
2 beaten eggs
1 tsp. salt
1/2 tsp. black pepper
1/4 tsp. dried oregano
1/4 tsp. dried thyme
3/4 cup marinara sauce
1/3 cup grated Parmesan cheese

Line a baking sheet with aluminum foil. Place the peppers on the baking sheet. Turn the oven to the broiler position. Broil the peppers for 8 minutes on each side or until they are charred. Remove the peppers from the oven and immediately place the peppers in a Ziploc bag. Let the peppers rest for 10 minutes.

Peel and seed the peppers. Pat the peppers dry with paper towels. Cut the peppers into thin strips. In a mixing bowl, add the ricotta cheese, Monterey Jack cheese, mozzarella cheese, eggs, salt, black pepper, oregano and thyme. Stir until well combined.

Spray a 9" square baking pan with non stick cooking spray. Place 1/3 of the peppers in the bottom of the baking pan. Spread 1/3 of the ricotta cheese mixture over the peppers. Spread 1/3 of the marinara sauce over the ricotta cheese. Repeat the layering process 2 more times. Sprinkle the Parmesan cheese over the top.

Preheat the oven to 350°. Bake for 30 minutes or until the casserole is golden brown. Remove the dish from the oven and serve.

Vegetable Cassoulet Casserole

Makes 6 servings

4 cups sliced mushrooms
2 tbs. olive oil
2 cups thinly sliced onion
1 garlic clove, minced
2 cups cubed zucchini
1 1/2 cups sliced yellow squash
4 cups cooked great northern beans, rinsed and drained
14 oz. can diced tomatoes
1/3 cup chopped parsley
1 tsp. dried basil
1/4 tsp. dried oregano
1/2 cup dry breadcrumbs
1 tsp. melted unsalted butter
2 cups shredded Swiss cheese

In a large skillet over medium heat, add the mushrooms, olive oil, onion and garlic. Saute the vegetables for 5 minutes. Add the zucchini and yellow squash to the skillet. Saute the squash for 5 minutes. Remove the skillet from the heat and stir in the great northern beans, tomatoes with juice, parsley, basil and oregano.

Preheat the oven to 350°. Spoon the vegetables and beans into a 2 quart casserole dish. In a small bowl, add the breadcrumbs and butter. Toss until the breadcrumbs are coated in the butter. Sprinkle the breadcrumbs over the top of the dish. Bake for 20 minutes. Sprinkle the Swiss cheese over the top of the casserole. Bake for 20 minutes or until the cheese is melted and the dish hot and bubbly. Remove the dish from the oven and serve.

Spanish Style Cauliflower Casserole

Makes 6 servings

1 head cauliflower
1 tsp. salt
1/4 cup unsalted butter, melted
1/2 tsp. black pepper
3/4 cup cracker crumbs
1/2 cup diced green pepper
16 oz. can tomatoes, diced
1 onion, chopped
1 1/2 cup shredded cheddar cheese

Remove the green outer leaves from the cauliflower and break the cauliflower into florets. Add the cauliflower to a dutch oven. Cover the cauliflower with water and place the pan over medium heat. Sprinkle 1/2 teaspoon salt over the cauliflower. Bring the cauliflower to a boil and cook for 5 minutes. Remove the pan from the heat and drain all the water from the cauliflower.

In a mixing bowl, add the butter, 1/2 teaspoon salt, black pepper and cracker crumbs. Toss until well combined. Add the green bell pepper, tomatoes with juice, onion, 1 1/4 cups cheddar cheese and cauliflower. Toss until all the ingredients are combined.

Preheat the oven to 350°. Pour the cauliflower mixture into a 2 quart casserole dish. Sprinkle 1/4 cup cheddar cheese over the top. Bake for 1 hour. Remove the dish from the oven and serve.

Broccoli Bean Casserole

Makes 6 servings

6 cups broccoli florets
1/2 cup chopped onion
2 garlic cloves, minced
3 tbs. unsalted butter
15 oz. can great northern beans, rinsed and drained
1/2 cup finely chopped roasted red bell peppers
1 tsp. dried oregano
1/2 tsp. salt
1/8 tsp. black pepper
2 cups shredded cheddar cheese
3 tbs. dry breadcrumbs

In a sauce pan over medium heat, add the broccoli. Cover the broccoli with water and bring the broccoli to a boil. Cook for 8 minutes or until the broccoli is crisp tender. Remove the pan from the heat and drain all the water from the broccoli.

In a skillet over medium heat, add the onion, garlic and 1 tablespoon butter. Saute the vegetables for 5 minutes. Remove the skillet from the heat. Spray a 11 x 7 casserole dish with non stick cooking spray. Spread the broccoli in the casserole dish. Spoon the onion and garlic over the broccoli. Spread the great northern beans and red bell peppers over the broccoli. Sprinkle the oregano, salt and black pepper over the broccoli. Sprinkle the cheddar cheese and breadcrumbs over the top of the casserole. Cut 2 tablespoons butter into small pieces and place over the breadcrumbs.

Preheat the oven to 350°. Bake for 20 minutes or until the casserole is hot and the cheese melted. Remove the dish from the oven and serve.

Potato Broccoli Cheese Bake

Makes 8 servings

2 tbs. unsalted butter
2 tbs. all purpose flour
2 cups whole milk
3 oz. pkg. cream cheese, cubed
1/2 cup shredded Swiss cheese
1 tsp. salt
1/8 tsp. ground nutmeg
1/8 tsp. black pepper
16 oz. pkg. frozen hash browns, thawed
10 oz. pkg. frozen chopped broccoli, thawed
1/4 cup dry seasoned breadcrumbs
1 tbs. melted unsalted butter

In a skillet over medium heat, add 2 tablespoons butter. When the butter melts, stir in the all purpose flour. Stir constantly and cook for 1 minute. Stir constantly and add the milk. Keep stirring and cook until the sauce thickens and bubbles. This will only take about 3-4 minutes.

Remove the pan from the heat and stir in the cream cheese, Swiss cheese, salt, nutmeg and black pepper. Stir until the cheeses melt. Add the hash browns and stir until combined.

Preheat the oven to 350°. Spray a 9" square pan with non stick cooking spray. Spread half of the potato mixture over the bottom of the pan. Spread the broccoli over the potatoes. Spoon the remaining potato mixture over the broccoli. Bake for 30 minutes.

Sprinkle the breadcrumbs over the top of the dish. Drizzle 1 tablespoon melted butter over the top of the breadcrumbs. Bake for 15 minutes. Remove the dish from the oven and serve.

Almond Broccoli Casserole

Makes 6 servings

6 cups fresh broccoli spears
2 cups water
1/3 cup slivered toasted almonds
2 tbs. melted unsalted butter
2 egg whites
1/2 cup mayonnaise
1/3 cup grated Parmesan cheese
1 tbs. grated onion

Add the broccoli and water to a sauce pan over medium heat. Bring the broccoli to a boil and place a lid on the pan. Cook the broccoli about 8 minutes or until the broccoli is tender. Remove the pan from the heat and drain all the water from the pan.

Preheat the oven to 450°. Spray an 8" square baking dish with non stick cooking spray. Place the broccoli spears in the baking dish. Sprinkle the almonds over the broccoli. Drizzle the butter over the broccoli.

In a mixing bowl, add the egg whites. Using a mixer on medium speed, beat the egg whites until soft peaks form. Add the mayonnaise, Parmesan cheese and onion. Mix only until combined. Spread the egg white mixture over the broccoli spears.

Bake for 6-8 minutes. The topping should be puffed and golden brown when ready. Remove the dish from the oven and serve immediately.

Broccoli Squash Casserole

Makes a 11 x 7 casserole dish

1 beaten egg
1 cup finely chopped onion
1 cup sour cream
10.75 oz. can cream of broccoli soup
2 cups cooked chopped broccoli
2 cups cooked chopped yellow squash
2 1/2 cups small seasoned croutons
4 cups shredded cheddar cheese
2 tbs. melted unsalted butter

In a mixing bowl, add the egg, onion, sour cream, cream of broccoli soup, broccoli, squash, 1 cup croutons and 2 cups cheddar cheese. Stir until combined. Spray a 11 x 7 casserole dish with non stick cooking spray. Spoon the casserole into the dish. Sprinkle 2 cups cheddar cheese over the top of the casserole.

In a small bowl, add 1 1/2 cups croutons and the butter. Toss until combined and sprinkle over the casserole. Bake for 30 minutes or until the casserole is hot and bubbly. Remove the dish from the oven and serve.

Broccoli Onion Deluxe

Makes 6 servings

6 cups fresh broccoli florets, cut into bite size pieces
2 onions, quartered
4 tbs. melted unsalted butter
2 tbs. all purpose flour
1 cup whole milk
3 oz. pkg. cream cheese, cubed
1/4 tsp. salt
1/8 tsp. black pepper
1/2 cup shredded sharp cheddar cheese
1 cup soft breadcrumbs

In a large sauce pan over medium heat, add the broccoli and onions. Add 1/2 cup water and place a lid on the pan. Cook the broccoli for 5 minutes. Remove the pan from the heat and drain all the water from the pan.

In a sauce pan over medium heat, add 2 tablespoons melted butter and the all purpose flour. Stir constantly and cook for 2 minutes. Add the milk and cook until the sauce thickens and bubbles. Remove the pan from the heat. Stir in the cream cheese, salt, black pepper and cheddar cheese. Stir until the cheese melts.

Preheat the oven to 350°. Spray a 2 quart casserole dish with non stick cooking spray. Add the broccoli and onion to the dish. Pour the cheese sauce over the broccoli. Sprinkle the breadcrumbs over the top. Drizzle 2 tablespoons melted butter over the breadcrumbs. Bake for 20 minutes. The dish should be hot, bubbly and the breadcrumbs golden brown. Remove the dish from the oven and serve.

Broccoli Macaroni Casserole

Makes 6 servings

Water
7 oz. pkg. elbow macaroni
3 tbs. unsalted butter
3 tbs. all purpose flour
1 1/2 tsp. salt
1/8 tsp. black pepper
1 1/2 cups whole milk
3/4 cup mayonnaise
2 cups cooked chopped broccoli
1 cup grated cheddar cheese

In a large sauce pan over medium heat, add 8 cups water. When the water boils, add the elbow macaroni. Cook the macaroni about 7 minutes or until the macaroni is tender. Remove the pan from the heat and drain all the water from the pan. Rinse the macaroni with cold water and drain all the water again.

In a sauce pan over medium heat, add the butter. When the butter melts, stir in the all purpose flour. Stir constantly and cook for 2 minutes. Add the salt, black pepper and milk. Stir constantly until the sauce begins to thicken. Stir in the mayonnaise and cook until the sauce thickens. Remove the pan from the heat.

Preheat the oven to 350°. Spray a 2 quart casserole dish with non stick cooking spray. Add the macaroni, sauce and broccoli to the casserole dish. Stir until combined. Sprinkle the cheddar cheese over the top of the dish. Bake for 20 minutes. The dish should be hot, bubbly and the cheese melted when ready.

Elegant Broccoli Dish

Makes 8 servings

1 1/2 cups water
1/4 cup plus 2 tbs. unsalted butter
6 oz. pkg. cornbread stuffing mix
2 pkgs. thawed frozen broccoli spears, 10 oz. size
2 tbs. all purpose flour
1 tsp. instant chicken bouillon granules
3/4 cup whole milk
3 oz. pkg. cream cheese, softened
1/4 tsp. salt
4 green onions, sliced
1 cup shredded cheddar cheese

In a sauce pan over medium heat, add the water, 1/4 cup butter and seasoning mix from the stuffing. Stir until well combined and bring the water to a full boil. Remove the pan from the heat and add the cornbread stuffing. Place a lid on the pan and let the stuffing sit for 5 minutes.

Spray a 9 x 13 baking dish with non stick cooking spray. Spoon the stuffing around the edges of the pan. Place the broccoli spears in the center of the dish. Spread the broccoli so it covers all the dish up to the stuffing.

In a sauce pan over low heat, add 2 tablespoons butter. When the butter melts, stir in the all purpose flour. Stir constantly and cook for 1 minute. Add the chicken bouillon granules and milk. Keep stirring until the sauce thickens and bubbles. Stir in the cream cheese and salt. Stir until the cream cheese melts and the sauce is smooth. Remove the pan from the heat. Spoon the sauce over the broccoli. Sprinkle the green onions and cheddar cheese over the top.

Preheat the oven to 350°. Cover the dish with aluminum foil or a lid. Bake for 35 minutes. Remove the aluminum foil and bake for 10 minutes. Remove the dish from the oven and serve.

Broccoli Bake

Makes 8 servings

8 cups fresh chopped broccoli
2 tbs. melted unsalted butter
1 tbs. vegetable oil
2 cups fresh mushrooms, finely chopped
1/4 cup minced onion
2 shallots, minced
4 eggs, beaten
2 egg yolks, beaten
1/2 cup fine dry breadcrumbs
1/2 cup whipping cream
1/8 tsp. ground nutmeg
Salt and black pepper to taste
Boiling water

In a sauce pan over medium heat, add the broccoli. Add 1 cup water to the sauce pan and place a lid on the pan. Cook the broccoli about 8 minutes or until the broccoli is tender. Remove the pan from the heat and drain all the water from the pan.

Add the broccoli to the blender. Process until smooth. Depending upon the size and strength of your blender, you may need to process the broccoli in batches.

In a skillet over medium heat, add the butter, vegetable oil, mushrooms, onion and shallots. Saute the vegetables for 5 minutes. Most of the liquid from the vegetables should be evaporated. Add the broccoli puree, eggs, egg yolks, breadcrumbs, whipping cream and nutmeg. Stir until well blended. Remove the pan from the heat. Season to taste with salt and black pepper.

Preheat the oven to 325°. Spray a 1 1/2 quart casserole dish with non stick cooking spray. Add the broccoli filling to the dish. Place the casserole dish in a roasting pan. Add boiling water to 1" in the roasting pan. Bake for 25 minutes. The broccoli should be set when ready. Remove the dish from the oven and serve.

Spinach Squares

Makes about 8 dozen

2 pkgs. thawed frozen chopped spinach, 10 oz. size
3 eggs, beaten
1/4 cup melted unsalted butter
1 cup all purpose flour
1 tsp. baking powder
1/2 tsp. season salt
1/4 tsp. black pepper
1 cup whole milk
4 cups shredded mozzarella cheese
2 tbs. chopped onion

Drain the spinach and press the spinach with paper towels to remove all the moisture. In a mixing bowl, add the eggs and butter. Whisk until well combined. Add the all purpose flour, baking powder, season salt, black pepper and milk. Whisk until well combined.

Stir in the spinach, mozzarella cheese and onion. Preheat the oven to 350°. Spray a 9 x 13 casserole dish with non stick cooking spray. Spoon the spinach into the casserole dish. Bake for 35 minutes. The dish should be lightly browned. Remove the dish from the oven and cool for 5 minutes. Cut into small squares and serve.

Tortellini Spinach Casserole

Makes 12 servings

12 cups water
2 pkgs. frozen cheese tortellini, 10 oz. size
8 cups sliced fresh mushrooms
1 tsp. garlic powder
1/4 tsp. onion powder
1/4 tsp. black pepper
1/2 cup unsalted butter
12 oz. can evaporated milk
8 oz. cheddar cheese, cubed
3 pkgs. frozen chopped spinach, 10 oz. size
2 cups shredded mozzarella cheese

Thaw the spinach at room temperature. Drain any moisture from the spinach. Pat the spinach dry with paper towels is needed. In a large dutch oven over medium heat, add the water. When the water is boiling, add the cheese tortellini. Cook for 3-5 minutes or until the tortellini are tender. Remove the pan from the heat and drain all the water from the pan.

In a large skillet over medium heat, add the mushrooms, garlic powder, onion powder, black pepper and butter. Saute the mushrooms for 10 minutes or until they are tender. Add the mushrooms to the tortellini.

Add the evaporated milk and cheddar cheese to the skillet. Stir constantly and cook until the cheese melts. Remove the skillet from the heat. Add the cheese sauce and spinach to the tortellini. Toss until all the ingredients are combined.

Spray a 9 x 13 casserole dish with non stick cooking spray. Spoon the casserole into the dish. Sprinkle the mozzarella cheese over the top. Preheat the oven to 350°. Bake for 20 minutes or until the casserole is hot and bubbly. Remove the dish from the oven and serve.

Cajun Spinach and Rice Casserole

Makes 6 servings

10 oz. pkg. frozen spinach, thawed and drained
1 tbs. Cajun seasoning
3 cups cooked rice
3 cups shredded cheddar cheese
1/4 cup melted unsalted butter
1 tsp. dried minced onion
4 eggs
1 cup whole milk
1 tsp. Worcestershire sauce
2 tsp. salt

Preheat the oven to 350°. Spray a 2 quart casserole dish with non stick cooking spray. Add the spinach, Cajun seasoning, rice, 2 cups cheddar cheese, butter and onion to the casserole dish. Stir until combined.

In a mixing bowl, add the eggs, milk, Worcestershire sauce and salt. Stir until combined and pour over the top of the casserole. Bake for 30 minutes. Sprinkle 1 cup cheddar cheese over the top of the casserole. Bake for 10 minutes or until the casserole is set, hot and bubbly. Remove the dish from the oven and serve.

Spinach Casserole

Makes 6 servings

2 pkgs. thawed frozen chopped spinach, 10 oz. size
1 cup water
6 oz. cream cheese, softened
2 tbs. unsalted butter, softened
2 tbs. grated Parmesan cheese

Add the spinach and water to a sauce pan over medium heat. Bring the spinach to a boil and place a lid on the pan. Cook the spinach for 6 minutes. Remove the pan from the heat and drain all the moisture from the spinach.

Preheat the oven to 350°. Spray a 1 quart casserole dish with non stick cooking spray. In a mixing bowl, add the cream cheese and butter. Whisk until well combined. Stir in the spinach and mix until combined. Spoon the spinach into the casserole dish. Sprinkle the Parmesan cheese over the top.

Place aluminum foil over the dish. Bake for 20 minutes. Remove the dish from the oven and serve.

Spinach Parmesan

Makes 6 servings

40 cups fresh spinach or about 4 lbs.
1/2 cup water
1/2 cup freshly grated Parmesan cheese
1/2 cup whipping cream
1/3 cup melted unsalted butter
1/3 cup finely chopped onion
1/8 tsp. black pepper
1/3 cup fine dry breadcrumbs

Remove the stems from the spinach and wash the spinach thoroughly. Add the spinach and water to a large dutch oven over medium heat. Place a lid on the pot and cook for 8 minutes. The spinach should be tender when ready. Remove the pot from the heat and drain all the liquid from the spinach.

Preheat the oven to 450°. Spray a 11 x 7 casserole dish with non stick cooking spray. Add the spinach, Parmesan cheese, whipping cream, butter, onion and black pepper to the casserole dish. Stir until well combined. Sprinkle the breadcrumbs over the top of the dish.

Bake for 15 minutes. The dish should be hot, bubbly and the breadcrumbs golden brown when ready. Remove the dish from the oven and serve.

Company Spinach

Makes 6 servings

2 pkgs. thawed frozen chopped spinach, 10 oz. size
1/3 cup chopped green onions
2 beaten eggs
1/4 cup melted unsalted butter
1/2 tsp. garlic powder
1/2 tsp. dried thyme
3 tomatoes, peeled and cut into 12 slices
1/2 tsp. garlic salt
1/4 tsp. black pepper
1/4 cup fine dry breadcrumbs
1/3 cup grated Parmesan cheese

Press the spinach with paper towels and remove all the moisture from the spinach. In a mixing bowl, add the spinach, green onions, egg, melted butter, garlic powder and thyme. Stir until combined.

Spray a 12 x 8 x 2 baking dish with non stick cooking spray. Preheat the oven to 350°. Place the tomato slices in the bottom of the baking dish. Sprinkle the garlic salt and black pepper over the tomatoes. Spoon the spinach mixture over the tomatoes. Sprinkle the breadcrumbs and Parmesan cheese over the top. Bake for 30 minutes.

The spinach should be tender and the dish hot and bubbly when ready. Remove the dish from the oven and serve.

Spinach Mushroom Casserole

Makes 6 servings

16 cups fresh spinach, washed and stems removed
1/2 cup chopped onion
1/4 cup unsalted butter
1/2 tsp. salt
1 cup whole button mushrooms, stems removed
1 cup shredded cheddar cheese

Add the spinach to a dutch oven over medium high heat. Place a lid on the pan and cook the spinach for 5 minutes. Do not add water to the spinach. Remove the pan from the heat and drain any liquid from the spinach. Chop the spinach and set aside for the moment.

In a skillet over medium heat, add the onion, 2 tablespoons butter and salt. Saute the onion for 5 minutes. Add the spinach and stir until combined. Spray a 1 quart casserole dish with non stick cooking spray. Preheat the oven to 350°. Spoon the spinach into the casserole dish.

In a skillet over medium heat, add 2 tablespoons butter and mushrooms. Saute the mushrooms for 6-8 minutes. The mushrooms should be browned and almost tender. Sprinkle 1/2 cup cheddar cheese over the top of the spinach in the casserole dish. Spoon the mushrooms and butter over the top of the cheese. Sprinkle the remaining 1/2 cup cheddar cheese over the top of the mushrooms.

Bake for 20 minutes. The dish should be hot and the mushrooms tender when ready. Remove the dish from the oven and serve.

Spinach Artichoke Casserole

Makes 6 servings

2 pkgs. thawed frozen spinach, 10 oz. size
1/2 cup unsalted butter
6 oz. cream cheese
8 oz. jar artichoke hearts, drained and chopped
1/4 tsp. black pepper
1 tbs. lemon juice
1 tbs. grated Parmesan cheese
1 tbs. seasoned breadcrumbs

In a sauce pan over medium heat, add the spinach. Add 1/2 cup water to the spinach and place a lid on the pan. Cook the spinach about 8 minutes or until the spinach is tender. Remove the pan from the heat and drain all the water from the spinach.

In a sauce pan over low heat, add the butter and cream cheese. Stir constantly and cook until the butter melts and the cream cheese softens. Remove the pan from the heat.

Spray a 2 quart casserole dish with non stick cooking spray. Preheat the oven to 325°. Add the spinach, butter mixture, artichokes, black pepper and lemon juice to the casserole dish. Stir until combined. Sprinkle the Parmesan cheese and breadcrumbs over the top. Bake for 30 minutes. The dish should be hot and bubbly when ready. Remove the dish from the oven and serve.

Spinach Ricotta Bake

Makes 6 servings

1/3 cup chopped green onions
1/2 tsp. dried basil
1/2 cup plus 2 tbs. melted unsalted butter
10 oz. pkg. frozen chopped spinach, thawed
2 cups crushed cracker crumbs
5 eggs, beaten
2 tbs. cold water
16 oz. carton ricotta cheese
1/2 cup shredded sharp cheddar cheese
1/4 tsp. salt
1/8 tsp. ground nutmeg
1 cup sour cream
2 tsp. lemon juice
1/2 cup chopped parsley

Drain the spinach of all moisture. Press the spinach with paper towels if needed. In a sauce pan over medium heat, add the green onions, basil and 2 tablespoons melted butter. Saute the onions for 3 minutes. Add the spinach and cook for 2 minutes. Remove the pan from the heat and set aside for now.

Preheat the oven to 375°. In a mixing bowl, add 1/2 cup butter, cracker crumbs, 1 beaten egg and cold water. Stir until combined. Press the mixture into a 12 x 8 x 2 baking dish. Press the crumbs over the bottom and sides of the dish. Bake for 10 minutes. Remove the crust from the oven and cool while you prepare the rest of the dish.

In a mixing bowl, add the ricotta cheese, 4 beaten eggs, cheddar cheese, salt and nutmeg. Whisk until well combined. Add the spinach mixture and stir until combined. Spoon the spinach mixture into the prepared crust. Bake for 30 minutes.

In a small bowl, stir together the sour cream and lemon juice. Spread the sour cream over the spinach. Sprinkle the parsley over the top. Bake for 10 minutes. Remove the dish from the oven and cool for 10 minutes before serving.

Spinach Cornbread Bake

Makes 6 servings

6 oz. pkg. corn muffin mix
2 eggs, beaten
1 cup sour cream
10.75 oz. can condensed French onion soup
10 oz. pkg. frozen chopped spinach, thawed
1/2 cup melted unsalted butter
1/2 cup shredded cheddar cheese

Drain all the liquid from the spinach. Press the spinach with paper towels if needed to remove the moisture. Spray a 12 x 8 x 2 casserole dish with non stick cooking spray. Preheat the oven to 350°.

In a mixing bowl, add the corn muffin mix, eggs, sour cream, French onion soup, spinach and butter. Stir until well combined. Spoon the mixture into the prepared dish. Bake for 25 minutes. The center of the dish should be set. Sprinkle the cheddar cheese over the top and bake for 5 minutes. Remove the dish from the oven and cool for 5 minutes before serving.

Overnight Cheesy Spinach Casserole

Makes 6 servings

2 pkgs. thawed frozen chopped spinach, 10 oz. size
1 cup sour cream
2 tbs. dry onion soup mix
1 cup shredded sharp cheddar cheese

In a sauce pan over medium heat, add the spinach. Add 1/2 cup water to the sauce pan and place a lid on the pan. Cook the spinach about 8 minutes or until the spinach is tender. Remove the pan from the heat and drain all the liquid from the spinach. Press the spinach with paper towels if needed. You want the spinach to be wet but not dripping in liquid.

Spoon the spinach into a 1 quart casserole dish. Add the sour cream and onion soup mix to the spinach. Stir until combined. Sprinkle the cheddar cheese over the top of the dish. Cover the dish with aluminum foil or a lid. Refrigerate the casserole overnight or at least 10 hours.

Remove the casserole from the refrigerator 45 minutes before you are ready to bake. Preheat the oven to 350°. Do not remove the cover and bake for 30 minutes. Remove the cover and bake for 5 minutes. The casserole should hot and bubbly when ready. Remove the dish from the oven and serve.

Brussels Sprouts & Artichoke Casserole

Makes 4 servings

1/2 cup water
10 oz. pkg. frozen brussels sprouts in butter, thawed
14 oz. can artichoke hearts, drained
1/2 cup mayonnaise
2 tsp. lemon juice
1/4 tsp. celery salt
1/4 cup grated Parmesan cheese
1/4 cup sliced almonds

In a sauce pan over medium heat, add the water. When the water is boiling, add the brussels sprouts. Cook the brussels sprouts for 6-7 minutes or until they are tender. Remove the pan from the heat and drain off all the liquid.

Spray a 1 quart casserole dish with non stick cooking spray. Preheat the oven to 325°. Spread the brussels sprouts and artichokes in the bottom of the casserole dish. In a mixing bowl, add the mayonnaise, lemon juice and celery salt. Stir until combined.

Spoon the mayonnaise mixture over the brussels sprouts and artichokes. Sprinkle the Parmesan cheese and almonds over the top. Bake for 25 minutes. The dish should be hot and the Parmesan cheese melted when ready. Remove the dish from the oven and serve.

Brussels Sprouts Casserole

Makes 4 servings

4 cups fresh brussels sprouts
1 cup water
1/4 cup chopped onion
2 tsp. melted unsalted butter
16 oz. can diced tomatoes with juice
1 tbs. cornstarch
1 tsp. dried basil
1/2 tsp. dry mustard
1/8 tsp. black pepper

Wash the brussels sprouts and remove any tough outer leaves. Cut the stem ends from the sprouts and make an X on the bottom of each brussels sprout. In a sauce pan over medium heat, add the brussels sprouts and water. Bring the water to a boil and cook for 6 minutes or until the brussels sprouts are tender. Remove the pan from the heat and drain all the water from the pan.

Place the sprouts in a 1 quart casserole dish. Preheat the oven to 350°. In a sauce pan over medium heat, add the onion and butter. Saute the onion for 4 minutes. Add the tomatoes with juice, cornstarch, basil, mustard and black pepper to the pan. Stir constantly and cook until the mixture thickens and bubbles. Remove the pan from the heat and pour the sauce over the brussels sprouts.

Cover the dish with aluminum foil. Bake for 30 minutes. Remove the dish from the oven and cool for 5 minutes before removing the aluminum foil.

Cheddar Kale Casserole

Makes 8 servings

2 pkgs. frozen chopped kale, 10 oz. size
1/4 cup water
1/4 cup plus 2 tbs. melted unsalted butter
1/4 cup all purpose flour
2 cups whole milk
1 cup shredded cheddar cheese
1 tsp. salt
1/8 tsp. black pepper
4 hard boiled eggs, chopped
1/2 cup seasoned breadcrumbs

In a sauce pan over medium heat, add the kale and water. Bring the kale to a boil and place a lid on the pan. Cook for 6-7 minutes or until the kale is tender. Remove the pan from the heat and drain all the liquid from the kale.

In a sauce pan over medium heat, add 1/4 cup melted butter and the all purpose flour. Stir constantly and cook for 2 minutes. Continue stirring and add the milk. Stir constantly and cook until the sauce thickens and bubbles. Add the cheddar cheese, salt and black pepper. Stir until the cheese melts. Remove the pan from the heat.

Preheat the oven to 350°. Spray a 1 1/2 quart casserole dish with non stick cooking spray. Add the kale, hard boiled eggs and cheese sauce to the casserole dish. Stir until combined. Sprinkle the breadcrumbs over the top of the dish. Drizzle 2 tablespoons butter over the breadcrumbs.

Bake for 30 minutes. The dish should be hot, bubbly and the breadcrumbs golden brown when ready. Remove the dish from the oven and serve.

Cheesy Swiss Chard

Makes 6 servings

12 cups Swiss chard leaves
1 tsp. salt
4 tbs. melted unsalted butter
2 tbs. all purpose flour
1/2 cup whole milk
8 oz. Velveeta cheese, cubed
1/2 cup dry seasoned breadcrumbs

You need 12 cups Swiss chard leaves after the stems are removed. This equals about 2 lbs. Swiss chard. Tear the leaves into bite size pieces. In a large dutch oven over medium heat, add the Swiss chard. Cover the Swiss chard with water and add 1/2 teaspoon salt. Bring the Swiss chard to a boil and place a lid on the pan. Cook for 5 minutes. Remove the pan from the heat and drain all the liquid from the pan. Press the leaves if needed to remove all the moisture from the Swiss chard.

In a sauce pan over medium low heat, add 2 tablespoons melted butter and the all purpose flour. Stir constantly and cook for 2 minutes. Continue stirring and add 1/2 teaspoon salt and the milk. Stir until the sauce thickens and bubbles. Add the Velveeta cheese and stir until the cheese melts. Remove the pan from the heat and stir until the cheese sauce is smooth and well combined.

Preheat the oven to 350°. Spray a 2 quart casserole dish with non stick cooking spray. Add the Swiss chard to the casserole dish. Pour the cheese sauce over the Swiss chard. Sprinkle the breadcrumbs over the top. Drizzle 2 tablespoons melted butter over the breadcrumbs. Bake for 25 minutes. The dish should be hot and bubbly when ready.

Creamy Cabbage Casserole

Makes 8 servings

8 cups cabbage, chopped
3 tbs. unsalted butter
1/4 cup all purpose flour
1/2 cup whole milk
1 cup whipping cream
1/2 tsp. salt
1/4 tsp. black pepper
1/8 tsp. ground nutmeg
1/4 cup grated Parmesan cheese
1/3 cup toasted breadcrumbs
2 tbs. melted unsalted butter

In a large sauce pan over medium heat, add the cabbage. Add 2 cups water to the sauce pan and bring the water to a boil. Simmer the cabbage about 10 minutes or until the cabbage is tender. Remove the pan from the heat and drain all the water from the cabbage.

In a sauce pan over low heat, add 3 tablespoons butter. When the butter melts, stir in the all purpose flour. Stir constantly and cook for 1 minute. Slowly add the whipping cream, salt, black pepper and nutmeg. Stir constantly and cook until the sauce thickens and bubbles. Remove the pan from the heat.

Preheat the oven to 375°. Spray a 1 1/2 quart casserole dish with non stick cooking spray. Add the cabbage and the cream sauce to the casserole dish. Stir until combined. Sprinkle the Parmesan cheese and breadcrumbs over the top of the casserole. Drizzle 2 tablespoons melted butter over the top of the dish.

Bake for 20 minutes or until the casserole is hot and bubbly. Remove the dish from the oven and serve.

Tex Mex Cabbage

Makes 6 servings

1 medium head cabbage
1 tsp. salt
2 tbs. unsalted butter
1 tbs. granulated sugar
1 onion, thinly sliced
1 green bell pepper, thinly sliced into rings
28 oz. can diced tomatoes, drained
1/4 tsp. black pepper
1/4 tsp. Tabasco sauce
1/4 cup shredded cheddar cheese

Remove the core from the cabbage and cut the cabbage into 6 wedges. Place the cabbage wedges in a sauce pan. Sprinkle 1/2 teaspoon salt over the cabbage. Cover the cabbage with water and place the pan over medium heat. Bring the cabbage to a boil and simmer for 10 minutes. Remove the pan from the heat and drain all the water from the pan.

Spray a 2 quart casserole dish with non stick cooking spray. Place the cabbage wedges in the casserole dish. In a sauce pan over medium heat, add the butter, granulated sugar, onion and green bell pepper. Saute the vegetables for 5 minutes. Add the tomatoes, 1/2 teaspoon salt, black pepper and Tabasco sauce. Stir until well combined and the mixture is thoroughly heated. Remove the pan from the heat and pour over the cabbage.

Preheat the oven to 375°. Sprinkle the cheddar cheese over the cabbage. Bake for 20 minutes. The dish should be hot. Remove the dish from the oven and serve.

Green Bean Garden Casserole

Makes 8 servings

1 large onion, sliced
1 red bell pepper, cut into thin strips
2 garlic cloves, minced
3 tbs. melted unsalted butter
1/4 cup all purpose flour
6 small baking potatoes, unpeeled and sliced
10 oz. pkg. frozen cut green beans, thawed
2 cups shredded Swiss cheese
1 cup half and half
1/2 tsp. dried rosemary
1/2 tsp. salt
1/4 tsp. black pepper

In a skillet over medium heat, add the onion, garlic, red bell pepper and butter. Saute the vegetables for 5 minutes. Sprinkle the all purpose flour over the vegetables. Stir constantly and cook for 1 minute. Remove the skillet from the heat.

Spray a 9 x 13 casserole dish with non stick cooking spray. Preheat the oven to 375°. Spoon half of the onion mixture in the casserole dish. Place half of the potato slices over the onion mixture. Spread half the green beans over the potatoes. Sprinkle half the Swiss cheese over the green beans. Repeat the layering process one more time using the remaining onion mixture, potato slices, green beans and Swiss cheese.

In a mixing bowl, add the half and half, rosemary, salt and black pepper. Stir until combined. Pour over the top of the casserole. Cover the dish with aluminum foil and bake for 1 hour. Remove the aluminum foil from the dish and bake for 10 minutes. Remove the dish from the oven and cool for 5 minutes before serving.

Green Beans Au Gratin

Makes 6 servings

4 cups fresh green beans, trimmed and washed
1/4 cup unsalted butter
1/4 cup all purpose flour
1 tsp. salt
1/8 tsp. dry mustard
1 1/2 cups whole milk
1/2 cup shredded Swiss cheese
1 1/2 tbs. grated Parmesan cheese
1/2 cup slivered almonds
Paprika to taste, optional

Cut the green beans into 1 1/2" pieces. Add the green beans to a sauce pan over medium heat. Cover the green beans with water. Bring the green beans to a boil and reduce the heat to low. Simmer the green beans for 20 minutes. Remove the pan from the heat and drain all the water from the pan.

In a sauce pan over medium heat, add the butter. When the butter melts, stir in the all purpose flour. Stir constantly and cook for 2 minutes. Keep stirring and add the salt, dry mustard and milk. Stir constantly until the sauce thickens and bubbles. Remove the pan from the heat and stir in the Swiss cheese and Parmesan cheese. Stir until the cheeses melt.

Preheat the oven to 350°. Spray a 1 1/2 quart casserole dish with non stick cooking spray. Add the green beans and cheese sauce to the casserole dish. Stir until combined. Sprinkle the almonds over the top. Sprinkle the paprika over the top if desired. Bake for 20 minutes. The dish should be hot and bubbly when ready. Remove the dish from the oven and serve.

Green Bean Surprise

Makes 6 servings

2 pkgs. frozen green beans, 10 oz. size
4 slices bacon, diced
2/3 cup chopped onion
1 tbs. all purpose flour
1 tbs. granulated sugar
1/2 cup whole milk
1/4 cup mayonnaise
1/4 cup shredded cheddar cheese
1/2 cup butter cracker crumbs

In a sauce pan over medium heat, add the green beans. Cover the green beans with water and bring to a boil. Place a lid on the pan and reduce the heat to low. Simmer the green beans about 20 minutes or until the green beans are tender. Remove the pan from the heat and drain all the water from the beans.

In a large skillet over medium heat, add the bacon. Cook the bacon about 7 minutes or until the bacon is crisp. Remove the bacon from the skillet and drain on paper towels. Leave the bacon drippings in the skillet. Crumble the bacon into pieces.

Add the onion to the skillet with the bacon drippings. Saute the onion for 5 minutes. Add the all purpose flour and granulated sugar. Stir constantly and cook for 1 minute. Add the milk and cook until the sauce thickens and bubbles.

Add the mayonnaise, green beans and bacon to the skillet. Stir until combined. Remove the skillet from the heat. Preheat the oven to 350°. Spray a 1 1/2 quart casserole dish with non stick cooking spray. Spoon the green beans and sauce into the dish. Sprinkle the cheddar cheese and cracker crumbs over the top. Bake for 20 minutes. Remove the dish from the oven and serve.

Green Beans with Sour Cream

Makes 8 servings

8 cups fresh green beans, trimmed and washed
1 onion, thinly sliced
2 tbs. fresh minced parsley
2 tbs. melted unsalted butter
2 tbs. all purpose flour
2 tsp. grated lemon zest
1 tsp. salt
1/4 tsp. black pepper
1 cup sour cream
1 cup buttered breadcrumbs

Cut the green beans into 1 1/2" pieces. Add the green beans to a large sauce pan over medium heat. Cover the green beans with water and place a lid on the pan. Simmer the green beans about 20 minutes or until the green beans are tender. Remove the pan from the heat and drain all the water from the pan.

In a skillet over medium heat, add the onion, parsley and melted butter. Stir frequently and cook for 4 minutes. The onion should be tender. Stir in the all purpose flour and cook for 1 minute. Stir in the lemon zest, salt and black pepper. Remove the skillet from the heat and stir in the sour cream.

Add the sour cream sauce to the green beans and stir until combined. Preheat the oven to 350°. Spoon the green beans into a 2 quart casserole dish. Sprinkle the breadcrumbs over the top. Bake for 20 minutes. Remove the dish from the oven and serve.

Asparagus Frittata Casserole

Makes 4 servings

3 eggs
1 1/2 cups whole milk
10 oz. pkg. frozen asparagus spears, thawed
1/2 cup shredded Monterey Jack cheese

Preheat the oven to 400°. Spray a 9" square baking pan with non stick cooking spray. In a mixing bowl, add the eggs and whole milk. Whisk until well combined and pour into the baking pan.

Drain any liquid from the asparagus spears. Place the asparagus spears over the eggs. Sprinkle the Monterey Jack cheese over the top. Bake for 15 minutes or until the center of the dish is set. The eggs should be set when ready. Remove the dish from the oven and serve.

Cheddar Asparagus Bake

Makes 8 servings

8 cups fresh asparagus, trimmed and washed
1 cup water
1/2 cup chopped onion
2 tbs. melted unsalted butter
2 tbs. all purpose flour
1 cup sour cream
1/4 tsp. salt
1/8 tsp. black pepper
2 cups shredded sharp cheddar cheese

In a sauce pan over medium heat, add the asparagus and water. Place a lid on the sauce pan and bring the asparagus to a boil. Cook the asparagus for 8 minutes or until the asparagus is tender. Remove the pan from the heat and drain all the water from the pan.

Place the asparagus in a 12 x 8 x 2 baking dish. In the sauce pan used to cook the asparagus, add the butter and onion. Saute the onion for 4 minutes. Sprinkle the all purpose flour over the onion. Stir constantly and cook for 2 minutes. Add the sour cream, salt and black pepper. Stir constantly and cook only until the sour cream is heated. Do not let the sauce boil. Remove the pan from the heat and pour the sauce over the asparagus.

Preheat the oven to 350°. Bake for 15 minutes. The sauce should be bubbly. Sprinkle the cheddar cheese over the top of the asparagus. Bake for 10 minutes or until the cheese is hot and melted. Remove the dish from the oven and serve.

Creamy Asparagus Casserole

Makes 6 servings

4 cups fresh asparagus spears
4 tbs. melted unsalted butter
2 tbs. all purpose flour
2 cups whole milk
1/2 tsp. salt
1/8 tsp. black pepper
4 hard boiled eggs, sliced
1/4 cup cracker crumbs

Trim the tough woody ends off the asparagus. Remove the tough outer peel. Cut the asparagus into 1 1/2 " pieces. In a large sauce pan over medium heat, add the asparagus spears. Cover the asparagus with water and bring to a boil. Simmer the asparagus about 6 minutes or until the asparagus is crisp tender. Remove the pan from the heat and drain all the water from the pan.

In a sauce pan over medium heat, add 2 tablespoons butter and the all purpose flour. Stir constantly and cook for 2 minutes. Add the milk, salt and black pepper. Stir constantly and cook until the sauce thickens and bubbles. Remove the pan from the heat and pour over the asparagus. Toss until the asparagus is coated in the sauce.

Preheat the oven to 350°. Spread half the asparagus and sauce over the bottom of an 8" square casserole dish. Place the egg slices over the asparagus. Spread the remaining asparagus and sauce over the eggs. Sprinkle the cracker crumbs over the top of the casserole. Drizzle 2 tablespoons butter over the cracker crumbs.

Bake for 30 minutes or until the dish is hot and bubbly. Remove the dish from the oven and serve.

White Cheddar Squash Casserole

Makes 8 servings

4 tbs. unsalted butter
1 cup chopped onion
12 cups yellow squash, sliced
2 tsp. salt
3/4 tsp. black pepper
2 tbs. all purpose flour
1 1/2 cups whole milk
2 1/2 cups shredded white cheddar cheese
2 tbs. Italian seasoned breadcrumbs

In a large skillet over medium heat, add 2 tablespoons butter and onion. Saute the onion for 5 minutes or until the onion is tender. Add the squash, 1 1/2 teaspoon salt and black pepper. Stir frequently and cook for 15 minutes or until the squash is tender. Remove the skillet from the heat.

In a sauce pan over medium heat, add 2 tablespoons butter. When the butter melts, stir in the all purpose flour. Stir constantly and cook for 2 minutes. Add the milk and 1/2 teaspoon salt. Stir constantly and cook until the sauce thickens and bubbles. Remove the pan from the heat and stir in the white cheddar cheese. Remove the pan from the heat.

Add the cheese sauce to the squash in the skillet. Stir until combined. Preheat the oven to 400°. Spray a 11 x 7 casserole dish with non stick cooking spray. Spoon the squash into the casserole dish. Sprinkle the breadcrumbs over the top. Bake for 20 minutes or until the dish is bubbly. Remove the casserole from the oven. Cool for 10 minutes before serving.

Green Chile Squash Casserole

Makes 4 servings

5 large yellow squash, sliced
1 1/2 tsp. salt
2 tbs. unsalted butter, softened
1 cup shredded cheddar cheese
1 onion, chopped
3 slices bacon, cooked and crumbled
2 oz. jar diced red pimento
2 tbs. chopped green chiles
1/4 tsp. garlic salt
1/8 tsp. black pepper
1/2 cup soft breadcrumbs
1 tbs. unsalted butter, melted

In a large sauce pan over medium heat, add the squash and 1 teaspoon salt. Cover the squash with water and cook about 8 minutes or until the squash are tender. Remove the pan from the heat and drain all the liquid from the squash. Using a potato masher or fork, mash the squash. Add 2 tablespoons softened butter, 1/2 teaspoon salt, cheddar cheese, onion, bacon, red pimento, green chiles, garlic salt and black pepper. Stir until combined.

Preheat the oven to 350°. Spray a 1 1/2 quart casserole dish with non stick cooking spray. Spoon the squash mixture into the casserole dish. Sprinkle the breadcrumbs over the casserole. Drizzle 1 tablespoon melted butter over the breadcrumbs.

Bake for 20 minutes or until the casserole is hot and bubbly. Remove the dish from the oven and serve.

Cheesy Squash Bake

Makes a 12 x 8 x 2 casserole dish

7 yellow summer squash, sliced
1 1/2 tsp. salt
2 eggs, separated
1 cup sour cream
2 tbs. all purpose flour
1 3/4 cups shredded cheddar cheese
8 slices bacon, cooked and crumbled
1/3 cup fine dry breadcrumbs
1 tbs. unsalted butter, melted

In a large sauce pan over medium heat, add the squash and 1 teaspoon salt. Cover the squash with water and cook about 8 minutes or until the squash are tender. Remove the pan from the heat and drain all the liquid from the squash. Sprinkle 1/2 teaspoon salt over the squash.

In a mixing bowl, add the egg yolks. Using a mixer on medium speed, beat the egg yolks for 2 minutes. Add the sour cream and all purpose flour to the egg yolks. Mix only until combined. In a separate mixing bowl, add the egg whites. Using a mixer on medium speed, beat until stiff peaks form. Fold the egg whites into the egg yolk mixture.

Spray a 12 x 8 x 2 casserole dish with non stick cooking spray. Preheat the oven to 350°. Spread half the squash in the casserole dish. Spread half the egg mixture over the squash. Sprinkle 3/4 cup cheddar cheese over the squash. Sprinkle the bacon over the top of the dish. Spread the remaining squash over the bacon. Spread the remaining egg mixture over the squash. Sprinkle 3/4 cup cheddar cheese over the squash.

In a small bowl, stir together the breadcrumbs and butter. Sprinkle the buttered breadcrumbs over the top of the casserole. Bake for 25 minutes or until the casserole is hot, bubbly and the top golden brown. Sprinkle 1/4 cup cheddar cheese over the casserole. Bake for 5 minutes. Remove the dish from the oven and cool for 5 minutes before serving.

Cheddar Parmesan Squash Casserole

Makes a 9 x 13 baking dish

8 cups sliced yellow squash
1 1/4 cups finely chopped onion
1 cup shredded cheddar cheese
1/2 cup chopped fresh chives
1 cup sour cream
1 tsp. garlic salt
1 tsp. black pepper
2 1/2 cups soft breadcrumbs
1 1/4 cups freshly shredded Parmesan cheese
2 tbs. unsalted butter, melted

Preheat the oven to 350°. Spray a 9 x 13 casserole dish with non stick cooking spray. In a sauce pan over medium heat, add the squash and onion. Cover the squash and onion with water. Bring the squash to a boil and cook for 8 minutes. The squash should be tender. Remove the pan from the heat and drain all the water from the pan.

Add the squash, cheddar cheese, chives, sour cream, garlic salt, black pepper, 1 cup breadcrumbs and 3/4 cup Parmesan cheese to the casserole dish. Stir until combined.

In a mixing bowl, add 1 1/2 cups breadcrumbs, 1/2 cup Parmesan cheese and butter. Stir until combined and sprinkle over the top of the casserole. Bake for 40 minutes or until the casserole is set and bubbly. Remove the dish from the oven and serve.

Zucchini Parmesan Bake

Makes 8 servings

9 cups sliced zucchini
2/3 cup chopped onion
1 cup sliced fresh mushrooms
3 tbs. vegetable oil
12 oz. can tomato paste
1 tsp. salt
1/2 tsp. garlic salt
1/8 tsp. black pepper
2/3 cup grated Parmesan cheese

In a large skillet over medium heat, add the zucchini, onion, mushrooms and vegetable oil. Saute the vegetables for 6 minutes. Remove the skillet from the heat. Stir in the tomato paste, salt, garlic salt, black pepper and 1/3 cup Parmesan cheese.

Spray a 2 quart casserole dish with non stick cooking spray. Preheat the oven to 350°. Spoon the zucchini into the casserole dish. Sprinkle 1/3 cup Parmesan cheese over the top of the dish. Cover the dish with a lid or aluminum foil. Bake for 30 minutes or until the zucchini are tender and the dish bubbly. Remove the dish from the oven and serve.

Eggplant Bake

Makes 8 servings

1 1/2 cups cooked brown rice
1 large eggplant, peeled and thinly sliced
6 oz. can tomato paste
1 cup cottage cheese
1 cup plain yogurt
3 tbs. water
3/4 tsp. dried basil
1/2 tsp. dried oregano
1/2 tsp. onion powder
1/2 tsp. garlic salt
1 cup shredded cheddar cheese
1 cup breadcrumbs
1 tbs. unsalted butter

Spray a 12 x 8 x 2 casserole dish with non stick cooking spray. Preheat the oven to 350°. Spread the rice in the bottom of the casserole dish. Place the eggplant slices over the rice.

In a small bowl, stir together the tomato paste, cottage cheese, yogurt, water, basil, oregano, onion powder and garlic salt. Spread the mixture over the eggplant slices. Sprinkle the cheddar cheese and breadcrumbs over the top of the casserole. Cut the butter into small pieces and place over the cheese and breadcrumbs.

Bake for 30 minutes or until the casserole is bubbly and the eggplant tender. Remove the dish from the oven and cool for 5 minutes before serving.

Nacho Eggplant Casserole

This is the only way I could get my kids to eat eggplant.

Makes 6 servings

2 eggplants, peeled and sliced 1/4" thick
2 eggs, well beaten
1 cup all purpose flour
2 tbs. vegetable oil
2 lbs. Velveeta cheese, cubed
2 cans diced tomatoes with green chiles, 10 oz. size
1/4 tsp. ground cumin

Pat the eggplant slices dry with a paper towel if needed. Add the eggs to a shallow bowl. Add the all purpose flour to a shallow bowl. Dip each eggplant slice into the egg allowing the excess egg to drip off back into the bowl. Dredge each slice in the all purpose flour.

You will need to cook the eggplant in batches. Eggplants soak up oil when cooking. Add additional oil if needed. In a skillet over medium heat, add the vegetable oil. When the oil is hot, add the eggplant slices. Cook about 1 minute on each side or until the eggplant is browned. The eggplant will not be cooked at this point. Remove the slices from the skillet and drain on paper towels. Drain any excess grease from the skillet.

Add the Velveeta, diced tomatoes with juice and cumin to the skillet. Stir constantly and cook until the cheese melts. Remove the skillet from the heat.

Preheat the oven to 350°. Spray a 9 x 13 casserole dish with non stick cooking spray. Cover the bottom of the dish with eggplant slices. Spoon 1/3 of the Velveeta cheese over the eggplant slices. Repeat the layering process 2 more times or until all the eggplant and cheese sauce are used.

Bake for 20 minutes or until the eggplant is tender and the dish bubbly. Remove the dish from the oven and serve.

Grits & Greens Breakfast Casserole

Makes a 9 x 13 baking dish

1 tsp. salt
1 1/2 cups quick cooking grits
4 cups water
1 cup shredded cheddar cheese
3 tbs. unsalted butter
1/2 cup half and half
1/4 tsp. cayenne pepper
10 eggs
3 cups cooked collard greens, drained
Tabasco sauce to taste, optional

Preheat the oven to 375°. Spray a 9 x 13 casserole dish with non stick cooking spray. In a sauce pan over medium heat, add the salt and water. When the water is boiling, stir in the grits. Stir frequently and cook the grits for 5 minutes. The grits should be thickened when ready. Remove the pan from the heat and stir in the cheddar cheese and butter. Stir until the cheese and butter melts.

In a mixing bowl, add the half and half, cayenne pepper and 2 eggs. Whisk until smooth and combined. Add the grits and collard greens to the bowl. Whisk until well combined. Season to taste with Tabasco sauce if desired. Spoon the grits and greens into the casserole dish.

Using the back of a large serving spoon, make 8 indentations in the grits. Break an egg in the center of each indentation. Bake for 15 minutes or until the eggs are cooked to your taste. Remove the dish from the oven and immediately cover the top of the dish with aluminum foil. Let the casserole sit for 10 minutes. Remove the aluminum foil and serve.

Hot Hominy Casserole

Try this as a side dish instead of potatoes or pasta.

Makes an 8 x 8 baking dish

2 cans drained yellow hominy, 15 oz. size
4 oz. can diced green chiles, drained
1/2 cup grated onion
1 cup sour cream
Salt and black pepper to taste
1 1/2 cups shredded sharp cheddar cheese
6 bacon slices, cooked and crumbled

Preheat the oven to 350°. Spray an 8 x 8 casserole dish with non stick cooking spray. Add the hominy, green chiles, onion and sour cream to the casserole dish. Stir until combined. Season to taste with salt and black pepper. Place a lid or aluminum foil on the dish. Bake for 20 minutes.

Sprinkle the cheddar cheese and bacon over the casserole. Bake for 10 minutes or until the cheese melts and the casserole is bubbly. Remove the dish from the oven and serve.

Scalloped Corn

Makes 5 servings

2 cups cooked fresh corn
2 eggs, beaten
1/4 cup green bell pepper, minced
1/2 tsp. salt
1 cup cracker crumbs
2 tbs. unsalted butter, cut into small pieces
2/3 cup half and half
Paprika to taste

Spray a 1 1/2 quart casserole dish with non stick cooking spray. Preheat the oven to 325°. In a mixing bowl, add the corn, eggs, green bell pepper and salt. Stir until well combined. Spoon half the mixture in the bottom of the casserole dish.

Sprinkle 1/2 cup cracker crumbs over the corn. Spread the remaining corn over the cracker crumbs. Sprinkle the remaining cracker crumbs over the corn. Pour the half and half over the top of the dish. Do not stir. Bake for 30 minutes or until the casserole is hot and bubbly. Remove the dish from the oven and sprinkle paprika to taste over the top of the casserole.

Fresh Corn Casserole

Makes 8 servings

6 slices bacon
4 cups frozen whole kernel corn
1 cup chopped green bell pepper
1/2 cup chopped onion
2 tomatoes, peeled and chopped
1 tsp. salt
1/4 tsp. black pepper

In a skillet over medium heat, add the bacon. Cook the bacon about 8 minutes or until the bacon is crisp. Remove the bacon from the skillet and drain on paper towels. Crumble the bacon into pieces.

Add the corn, green bell pepper and onion to the skillet. Saute the vegetables for 5 minutes or until the onion and green bell pepper are tender. Remove the skillet from the heat. Add the tomatoes, bacon, salt and black pepper to the skillet. Stir until combined.

Preheat the oven to 350°. Spray a 2 quart casserole dish with non stick cooking spray. Spoon the corn mixture into the dish. Bake for 20 minutes or until the corn is tender. Remove the dish from the oven and serve.

Corn and Tomato Casserole

Makes 8 servings

8 slices bacon, cut in half
2 cups soft breadcrumbs
2 cups peeled and chopped fresh tomatoes
1 green bell pepper, chopped
3 cups frozen whole kernel corn, thawed
1/4 tsp. salt
1/4 tsp. granulated sugar
1/4 tsp. black pepper
1/4 cup unsalted butter, melted

Preheat the oven to 375°. Place half the bacon slices in a shallow 2 quart casserole dish. Sprinkle 1 cup breadcrumbs over the bacon. Place 1 cup tomatoes and half the green bell pepper over the breadcrumbs. Place 1 1/2 cups corn over the vegetables. Sprinkle 1/8 teaspoon salt, 1/8 teaspoon granulated sugar and 1/8 teaspoon black pepper over the vegetables.

Place 1 cup tomatoes, remaining green bell pepper and 1 1/2 cups corn over the top of the casserole. Sprinkle 1/8 teaspoon salt, 1/8 teaspoon granulated sugar and 1/8 teaspoon black pepper over the vegetables.

In a small bowl, toss together the butter and 1 cup breadcrumbs. Sprinkle the buttered breadcrumbs over the top of the casserole. Place the remaining bacon slices over the top of the casserole. Bake for 45 minutes or until the bacon is done and crispy, the corn tender and the casserole golden brown. Remove the casserole from the oven and serve.

Corn and Cheese Casserole

Makes 4 servings

2 cups frozen whole kernel corn, thawed
1 cup shredded sharp cheddar cheese
1 cup soft breadcrumbs
1/4 cup chopped green bell pepper
1/3 cup whole milk
2 tbs. unsalted butter, melted
1 tbs. dried minced onion
1 tsp. salt
1/4 tsp. ground ginger
1/8 tsp. black pepper

Preheat the oven to 350°. Spray a 1 quart casserole dish with non stick cooking spray. Add all the ingredients to the casserole dish. Stir until well combined. Cover the casserole dish with a lid or aluminum foil.

Bake for 35 minutes or until the corn is tender. Remove the casserole from the oven and serve.

Cheesy Pimento Corn Casserole

Makes 8 servings

2 tbs. unsalted butter
1/2 cup chopped onion
2 garlic cloves, minced
4 cups shredded white cheddar cheese
2 cans drained whole kernel corn, 15 oz. size
14 oz. can cream style corn
1 cup sour cream
4 oz. jar diced red pimentos, drained
1/2 cup self rising yellow cornmeal

In a skillet over medium heat, add the butter. When the butter melts, add the onion and garlic. Saute the onion for 5 minutes. Remove the skillet from the heat.

Add the white cheddar cheese, whole kernel corn, cream style corn, sour cream, red pimentos and cornmeal to the skillet. Stir until all the ingredients are combined.

Preheat the oven to 350°. Spray a 11 x 7 casserole dish with non stick cooking spray. Spoon the casserole into the dish. Bake for 50 minutes or until the center of the casserole is set. Remove the casserole from the oven and cool for 10 minutes before serving.

Chipotle Rice Casserole

Makes 4 servings

1/2 cup dry long grain rice
1 cup water
7 oz. jar roasted red bell peppers, drained and chopped
15 oz. can black beans, rinsed and drained
11 oz. can Mexicorn, drained
14 oz. can diced tomatoes, drained
1 tbs. chopped fresh cilantro
1 tbs. canned chipotle peppers in adobo, chopped
1 cup shredded Pepper Jack cheese
3 tbs. vegetable oil
1/4 cup all purpose flour
1 cup whole milk
1/2 cup chicken broth
1 tsp. ground cumin
1 tsp. garlic salt
2 Roma tomatoes, sliced

In a sauce pan over medium heat, add the rice and water. When the rice is boiling, reduce the heat to low. Place a lid on the pan. Simmer the rice for 15 minutes or until the rice is tender. Remove the pan from the heat and let the rice sit for 5 minutes.

Spray an 8" square casserole dish with non stick cooking spray. Preheat the oven to 350°. In a mixing bowl, add the rice, roasted red bell peppers, black beans, Mexicorn, diced tomatoes, cilantro, chipotle peppers and 1/2 cup Pepper Jack cheese. Stir until combined and spoon into the casserole dish.

In a sauce pan over low heat, add the vegetable oil and all purpose flour. Whisk until well combined. Stir constantly and cook for 2 minutes or until the flour is smooth and bubbly. Add the milk, chicken broth, cumin and garlic salt. Stir constantly and cook until the sauce thickens and bubbles. Remove the pan from the heat and stir in 1/2 cup Pepper Jack cheese. Pour the sauce over the rice and vegetables in the casserole dish.

Bake for 25 minutes or until the casserole is hot and bubbly. Remove the dish from the oven and place the Roma tomato slices over the top before serving.

Tomato Casserole

Makes 6 servings

2 cans diced tomatoes, 15 oz. size, drained
1 1/2 cups soft breadcrumbs
1/4 cup unsalted butter, melted
1/4 cup light brown sugar
1/4 tsp. black pepper

Preheat the oven to 400°. Spray a 9" square baking dish with non stick cooking spray. Add all the ingredients to the baking dish. Stir until combined. Bake for 35 minutes. The casserole should be hot and bubbly when ready.

Remove the dish from the oven and serve.

Okra Tomato Bake

Makes 6 servings

8 slices bacon, cut into small pieces
1 onion, finely chopped
10 oz. pkg. frozen cut okra, thawed
1 green bell pepper, finely chopped
2 tbs. instant rice
16 oz. can diced tomatoes
1 tbs. granulated sugar
Pinch of garlic salt
1/4 tsp. salt
1/8 tsp. black pepper
1 tbs. grated Parmesan cheese
1/4 cup fine dry breadcrumbs
1 tbs. unsalted butter, melted

Add the bacon to a skillet over medium heat. Cook the bacon about 6 minutes or until the bacon is done and crispy. Remove the bacon from the skillet and drain on paper towels.

Add the onion and okra to the skillet. Stir frequently and cook about 6 minutes or until the onion is lightly browned. Remove the skillet from the heat and drain the onion and okra on paper towels.

Spray a 1 1/2 quart casserole dish with non stick cooking spray. Preheat the oven to 350°. Add the bacon, onion and okra, green bell pepper and rice to the casserole dish. Stir until combined.

In a blender, add the tomatoes with juice, granulated sugar, garlic salt, salt and black pepper. Process until smooth and pour over the top of the casserole. Sprinkle the Parmesan cheese over the top of the dish. Sprinkle the breadcrumbs over the top of the casserole. Drizzle the butter over the breadcrumbs.

Bake for 45 minutes. Remove the dish from the oven and serve.

Bacon, Black Eye Pea & Rice Casserole

Makes 4 servings

2 pkgs. frozen black eye peas, 10 oz. size
1 cup chopped onion
4 cups water
1 tbs. salt
2/3 cup rice
10 slices bacon, diced
2/3 cup barbecue sauce
1/4 tsp. black pepper
2 tbs. bacon drippings

In a sauce pan over medium heat, add the black eye peas, onion, water and salt. Bring the peas to a boil and reduce the heat to low. Simmer the peas for 30 minutes. Add the rice and simmer the rice for 20 minutes. Stir occasionally while the rice and peas are cooking. Remove the pan from the heat.

In a skillet over medium heat, add the bacon. Cook the bacon about 8 minutes or until the bacon is done but not crispy. Remove the skillet from the heat and remove the bacon from the skillet. Drain the bacon on paper towels.

Preheat the oven to 350°. Spray a 2 quart casserole dish with non stick cooking spray. Add the peas and rice, barbecue sauce, black pepper, half the bacon and bacon drippings to a 2 quart casserole dish. Stir until well combined. Sprinkle the remaining bacon over the top.

Bake for 30 minutes or until the dish is hot and bubbly. The bacon on top should be crispy. Remove the dish from the oven and serve.

CHAPTER INDEX

Ham & Sausages

Tuna & Seafood

Beans, Vegetables, Sides & Meatless Casseroles

Beans, Vegetables, Sides & Meatless Casseroles cont'd

ABOUT THE AUTHOR

Lifelong southerner who lives in Bowling Green, KY. Priorities in life are God, family and pets. I love to cook, garden and feed most any stray animal that walks into my yard. I love old cookbooks and cookie jars. Huge NBA fan who loves to spend hours watching basketball games. Enjoy cooking for family and friends and hosting parties and reunions. Can't wait each year to build gingerbread houses for the kids.

Made in the USA
Las Vegas, NV
19 March 2025

19826418R00104